# This Tender Place

Terrace Books, a division of the University of Wisconsin Press,
takes its name from the Memorial Union Terrace, located at
the University of Wisconsin–Madison. Since its inception in 1907,
the Wisconsin Union has provided a venue for students, faculty, staff,
and alumni to debate art, music, politics, and the issues of the day.
It is a place where theater, music, drama, dance, outdoor activities,
and major speakers are made available to the campus and the community.
To learn more about the Union, visit www.union.wisc.edu.

# This Tender Place

## *The Story of a Wetland Year*

*Autumn* *Winter*

*Summer* *Spring*

# Laurie Lawlor

**TERRACE BOOKS**
A trade imprint of the University of Wisconsin Press

Terrace Books
A trade imprint of the University of Wisconsin Press
1930 Monroe Street
Madison, Wisconsin 53711

www.wisc.edu/wisconsinpress/

3 Henrietta Street
London WC2E 8LU, England

3     5     4     2

Printed in the United States of America

Library of Congress Cataloging-in-Publication Data
Lawlor, Laurie.
This tender place: the story of a wetland year / Laurie Lawlor.
        p.        cm.
Includes bibliographical references.
ISBN 0-299-21460-5 (cloth: alk. paper)
1. Lawlor, Laurie.   2. Wetlands—Wisconsin—Anecdotes.
3. Natural history—Wisconsin—Anecdotes.   I. Title.
        QH87.3.L39        2005
    578.768′09775—dc22        2005005447

ISBN 0-299-21464-8 (pbk.: alk. paper)

FOR MY FATHER

Running water never disappointed.
Crossing water always furthered something.
Stepping stones were stations of the soul.

A kesh could mean the track some called a causey
Raised above the wetness of the bog.
Or the cause where it bridged old drains and streams.

It steadies me to tell these things. Also
I cannot mention keshes or the ford
Without my father's shade appearing to me.

On a path towards sunset, eyeing spades and clothes
That turf cutters stowed perhaps or souls cast off
Before they crossed the log that spans the burn.

Seamus Heaney from "Crossings" in Seeing Things

# Contents

# Illustrations

# Preface and
## Acknowledgments

〜〜〜〜〜〜〜〜〜〜〜

I enter a swamp as sacred space.

Henry David Thoreau, *Walking*

Small lakes wander across the topographical map of southeastern
Wisconsin like the tracks of an enormous, heavy-footed beast. Here
and there meander streams and rivers careless as tail-drag. Who
made these land forms? Stare long enough at the map and the great
monster-creator appears. It pauses; scatters bits of feather, bones,
drops of blood; then lumbers northeast toward Lake Michigan.

Among the trail of paw prints sunk deep into the earth is a small
lake that appears as tentative as a toe mark jammed against the low
hills. This thirty-acre body of water empties into a crooked stream
flowing north. Another stream enters the lake to the south. Extending east and west beyond this stream stretches a pristine sedge
meadow and fen nourished by mineral-rich springs.

In this wetland my journey began.

The first time I stumbled into this place was July 1994. I was still
full of grief and sadness. Eight months earlier my father had died of
lung cancer. That same year, after a long battle with emphysema, my
father-in-law succumbed to a stroke and died. My family was in a
shambles. We decided to look for a piece of land in the country; it
seemed a way to reconstruct ourselves, my husband and I agreed. A
way to refocus. Our teenage children were less than enthusiastic, but
we ignored their protests and launched into a rural real estate search
that soon appeared doomed.

The houses we could afford were mostly desperate, dilapidated
places. Advertised as "rustic farmettes," they featured such dubious
charms as crusty refried beans caked on the stoves, abandoned autos

and farm machinery rusting in the back yards, collapsing barns, and fierce German shepherds living next door.

This was not the reconstruction I had in mind.

We were about to give up when we received a phone call. "Come look at the place," the realtor begged. "Eleven acres. Needs some work, but the price is right."

I drove up. Her assessment of the house proved far rosier than the reality. The place was a nightmare of Brady Bunch–era decorating ravaged by neglect and abuse—the aftershock of a rancorous divorce. The house reeked of rancid grease, stale pipe smoke, and cat litter. Grime coated the windows. The roof leaked and the walls, doors, and floors had been brutally scratched, gouged, and in some places kicked.

I turned to leave. "Go out back," the realtor said. "There's a path that leads to the stream that connects to the lake."

Reluctantly, I wandered behind the house. In the distance I could see shimmering water. All I had to do was find the stream. I walked down the hill and entered a path surrounded by overgrown shrubs and small trees. Beyond from some hidden place came the calls of unfamiliar birds. Their wild, clattering sound made me shiver.

I kept walking, and the trees began to disappear. Now I was surrounded by cattails with bobbing, brown, sausage-like heads. Long, spear-shaped leaves arched over the path and swiped me in the eyes. The path turned soft, treacherous, and wet. I sank ankle-deep into the black ooze. When I struggled to pull out my feet, I was assailed by the ripe odor of rotten egg, decaying leaves, old clothes, and wet dog.

Mud plundered my shoes, caked my legs. Where was the stream? Now that I'd ruined my clothes and shoes, I did not want to return without seeing what I'd come to see. I trudged onward, eyes downcast. I had to concentrate on every step to keep from making a wrong move and being sucked under.

The path seemed to go on forever.

Finally, I found the bend where the stream curved among tall reeds. Cold water seeped up to my knees. I stood beside an overturned canoe in a small clearing among the cattails and tried to peer out at the current. On the water floated a riot of tangled green plants. I was no expert but the place certainly did not look promising.

Whenever I moved, my feet churned up an even stronger smell of rotten eggs. How could anyone reach the lake from here?

Hot, sweaty, and filthy, I decided to go back and tell the realtor once again that this was definitely not the place we wanted.

I turned. And for the first time I scanned south beyond the cattails. Alive with wind, the marsh sedges moved like a great ocean. Above the green-swept openness arched blue sky.

And at that moment I felt a kind of awe. This was a mysterious, secret place without a house or another person in sight. I felt as surprised and enthralled as the children who pushed through the back of the wardrobe in *The Lion, the Witch, and the Wardrobe* and discovered a whole new world. I was struck by boundlessness and the incomparable grassy smell of distance. I could be free here. Perhaps I could even be happy.

Muddy and wet but strangely revived, I trudged back up the path to the hideous house to tell the realtor we'd make an offer. As soon as I said the words, I wondered how I'd convince my family. How could I describe the value of owning a house purely for the wet, muddy openness in the back—complete with a boat landing with no easy access and a canoe with no paddles? Here was something I could not really understand except that I knew it was a good idea. We needed to buy this tender place, this piece of swamp.

To my delight and amazement, my normally rational husband was equally swept away by the land behind the house. Our children, however, were anything but enchanted; my daughter burst into tears when she saw the place, and my son fumed darkly that we had lost our minds.

In spite of their protests, we went ahead and bought the property. Four months later, after a frenzy of cleaning, we managed to make the place barely presentable. On a bright clear afternoon in late November, exactly a year after my father's death, we took his ashes and buried them beneath a pin oak we planted near the edge of the wetland. Everyone agreed it was a resting place preferable to the shelf in the funeral parlor closet where his ashes had remained since the cremation because no one could decide what to do next.

My mother and five brothers and sisters and their families gathered in a rare, harmonious circle around the tree. Each person had a chance to say something about the past year. It was a windy, tearful day. The entire time, a line from Wendell Berry's "Three Elegiac Poems" kept running through my mind: "He's hidden among all that is / And cannot be lost."

When we finished tamping down the earth around the tree, a high-pitched call echoed from the wetland. One of my sisters turned to me and asked, "Who's that?"

"I don't know," I said.

"You should find out. Sounds like it's going to be Dad's new neighbor."

She was right. There were so many things about this place and its inhabitants I knew nothing about, so many things I needed to understand.

This is the story of a wetland year and what I discovered about plants and animals, fire and water, humans and insects, refuge and renewal.

I am not a biologist or plant expert. My knowledge is what writer Barry Lopez calls "intimate rather than encyclopedic, human but not necessarily scholarly." What I hope to share are some of the details of a decade of experience living beside this tender place—a landscape of abundant, sometimes inaccessible, beauty that has been often ignored or misunderstood.

This is a personal record of what I've seen, heard, smelled, and felt in all seasons, all weathers, all times of day. With an uncalculating mind and an attitude of regard, I have attempted to embrace the wetland from all angles—above, below, north, south, east, west. To sense the variety of its plants, its animals, I have examined the sky, submerged underwater, plunged into mud, peered between sedges, and poked beneath stumps.

And yet no matter how hard I've tried to use my eyes, ears, nose, tongue, body, mind to comprehend the landscape, I sense that much will always remain stubbornly hidden.

This book by its very nature is incomplete. Like all places worth investigating, the wetland refuses to easily give up its secrets. So much abides in mystery. And that is only fitting. As Henry David Thoreau wrote, "How long may we have gazed upon a particular scenery and think that we have seen and known it, when, at length,

Early mist hovers on the fen with the lake in the distance.

some bird or quadruped comes and takes possession of it before our eyes, and imparts to it a wholly new character."

Every day, every season, every year imparts a wholly new character to my investigation. My education is never-ending.

Special thanks go to the late Jane Jordan Browne, my literary agent, who enthusiastically worked to preserve Wisconsin land and history throughout her life. Thanks also goes to: William Baum and Barbara Vitkovits, Lee Baum Belfield, Randall and Jane Craig, Jack and Marcia Boeing, Jerry Emmerich, and the Nature Conservancy Wisconsin Chapter staff, especially Scott Thompson, Director of Conservation–Eastern Wisconsin; Sandy Woken, Mukwonago Program Assistant; Nancy Braker; Hannah Spaul, and the numerous fire team volunteers. I'd also like to recognize the assistance of Lee Clayton of the Wisconsin Geological and Natural History Survey, Rob Nurre of the Board of Commissioners of Wisconsin Public Lands, the librarians at the Wisconsin Historical Society Archives Department, and Becky Briggs of the Whitewater Area Research Center. Thanks go to marvelous marsh explorers Ruby and Cole Thompson and the rest my family. This book would not be possible without the enthusiasm and patience of my children, Megan and John Patrick, and the loving support and unfailing sense of humor of my husband, Jack.

Unless noted, I have taken all photographs. I thank William Baum for allowing me to use the photo on page 143.

# *Introduction*

In the beginning the Earth was in constant motion, according to the Ho-Chunk (formerly called the Winnebago). These early Wisconsin residents say that Earthmaker threw down grass and trees to stabilize the land. He scattered every kind of vegetation. But even this could not keep the Earth from pitching and rocking in all directions. Finally, Earthmaker took the four corners of the land and drove deep into each corner a snakelike water spirit to hold the land steady. And the water spirits held fast. Without them, all would return to chaos and reckless motion again.

Water and water spirits continue to hold fast here. Water seen and unseen—in the sky, on the land, and deep underground. What the Ho-Chunk and so many indigenous people have understood about the Midwestern wetland landscape is the power that water has had to give life or take it away. Water is both benign and dangerous, benevolent and merciless, comforting and calamitous. It is a source of life that can never be taken for granted, never be abused without serious consequences.

Among the Ho-Chunk is the belief that springs are the openings or entrances through which animals enter the spirit world. In 1926 elderly Ho-Chunk Oliver LeMere spoke with historian Charles E. Brown in Madison, Wisconsin. LeMere explained to Brown how his ancestors treated springs as sacred places that required offerings of tobacco and other articles. Likewise, no Ho-Chunk would think of crossing a lake in a canoe without first making some kind of offering. Springs and other bodies of water, LeMere said, were in the special care of members of the water spirit clan, one of a dozen family groupings that organized community life among the Ho-Chunk.

The water spirit is a powerful image. There's a certain fierceness in the various forms it takes in early legends and iconography. The old people, according to LeMere, spoke of a "long-tailed animal with horns on its head, great jaws and claws and a body like a big snake." LeMere said that few people saw this creature except at night. "But its presence in the river was known by the churning and boiling of the water."

When I began my search to understand this wetland, I suspected that everything I'd come here to find was concealed in the world of water. I like to think of the Ho-Chunk water spirit as a kind of guardian of the landscape. Understanding and respecting the role of water seems key to understanding the workings and the importance of wetlands.

By its very definition wetlands are water wed to land. Officially, the U.S. Fish and Wildlife Service defines a wetland as "lands transitional between terrestrial and aquatic systems where the water table is usually at or near the surface or the land is covered by shallow water." Simply put, a wetland, writes conservationist Jim Zimmerman, "is where you can get your feet wet but can't swim." It is land that must be wet enough or flooded frequently enough to provide the right environment for special wetland vegetation.

Almost anywhere in North America, it's possible to find some type of freshwater wetland. A *marsh* is characterized by bulrushes, cattails, arrowhead, bur-reed—all of which can have their roots submerged. *Bogs* feature a spongy carpet of sphagnum moss over a thick layer of peat. Bogs are isolated from nutrient-giving groundwater and are fed only by rain water. *Sedge meadows* are inhabited by grass-like plants called sedges, which flourish in soil saturated but not necessarily submerged by water. *Fens,* among the rarest wetlands, are fed by underground limestone springs, which help give the soil a special alkaline quality.

Some small wetlands are marshy areas along the edges of forest preserve lakes, others border moving streams. Recently, many new suburban housing developments have been required by law to

Thick stands of cattails surround the stream that empties into a small, pristine lake.

include open space for flood runoff, creating areas which often look very much like wetlands during certain times of the year.

Wetlands are considered the most productive ecosystem in the world. A freshwater marsh, for example, produces 4.4 pounds (2 kilograms) of biomass per 11 square feet per year. This makes a wetland more productive in terms of plant growth than agricultural or natural grassland. As storehouses of biodiversity, wetlands serve as irreplaceable habitats for wildlife, especially migrating waterfowl. Wetlands provide food and shelter for 39 percent of all Wisconsin bird species and for about 45 percent of all animal species nationwide, many of which are threatened or endangered.

What we often forget or overlook in living in modern houses and apartments with faucets that spout seemingly unlimited fresh water is the origin of water—where it comes from and how it is renewed. Many people do not realize that wetlands play an intrinsic, often invisible role in the health of a community's water sources.

In Wisconsin, as in so many places around the country, readily available fresh water is becoming rarer and rarer. Wetlands are of tremendous importance as water storage sites that act as sponges after heavy rains and snow melt. Wetlands hold flood water. Wetland plants and animals filter out pollutants and sediments, then allow water to slowly seep back into the ground to recharge, or replenish, underground aquifers or reservoirs.

As the population skyrockets and demands for drinking water, irrigation, sewage lines, and lawn watering increases, fresh water reserves locked in readily available, shallow aquifers are being quickly tapped out. Millions of people depend on a sandstone aquifer located near the Illinois-Wisconsin border. As water is extracted from the aquifer at an unsustainable rate—far faster than it can be replenished by rain or snowmelt—it will eventually be unable to transmit water to well fields. As the aquifer is pumped dry, water will become increasingly more expensive to draw. Deeper pumping operations mean more contaminants and undesirable undissolved minerals—and more expense. Another danger of aquifer depletion is that eventually the cavity can collapse.

Yet in spite of the myriad helpful jobs wetlands perform, they are endangered landscapes.

Economic pressure exists to drain wetlands for so-called practical use—another housing complex, another resort, another shopping mall, another parking lot, another acre of corn or soybeans. An estimated 500,000 acres of wetland vanish each year. In the past 200 years, more than half of the original wetlands in the lower forty-eight states has been drained, ditched, plowed under or built over. In the 1780s an estimated 211 to 221 million acres of wetlands existed in what's now the continental United States. Two hundred years later, only 104 million acres remain—a loss of 53 percent. In Wisconsin just 5.3 of the original 9.8 million acres of wetland have survived.

Once drained and destroyed, a biodiverse wetland can never fully be reclaimed or reintroduced. "No space craft," naturalist John Madson writes, "can take us where it has gone."

The small, unspoiled wetland I live beside is unique because it contains a fen, one of the rarest wetland types in North America. Only 120 of these high quality, spring-fed, calcium-rich preserves exist in the United States. The Southeast Wisconsin Regional Planning Commission recently named this fen the most biologically diverse in southeast Wisconsin. Surrounded by agricultural "tame-land" in Walworth County, one of the fastest growing counties in the region, the wetland is a rare wonder that survived mainly because of incredible luck and the devotion of a handful of landowners.

And yet this wetland faces the continuous danger that it, too, may one day disappear.

Even as I write this, I can hear the engine roar and beeping reverse squeal of a backhoe across the road as it tears through a grove of bur oak to create another new asphalt-paved road to another house. The sound sickens me because I know that the house will be built on a ridge above the stream where the beavers have built their dam, opposite the culvert that allows water into the heart of the fen. Water clouded by silt can irrevocably change the quality of life in wetland plants and animals.

Whenever a wetland is threatened, I take comfort in the notion of an indomitable water spirit with great jaws, claws, and serpentine body—the protector of all wetlands. I wish such fierceness was better known. Perhaps then land developers might think twice about digging and ditching and draining and paving. Would we have second thoughts about destroying wetlands if we better understood and appreciated, as the Ho-Chunk did, that water spirits are all that stands between stability and reckless chaos?

*This Tender Place*

# Winter

But the water, married to the stone,
voluble, though frozen; the water
even when and though frozen
still whispers and moans—
William Carlos Williams,
"Paterson: The Falls"

# December

Wind whips across the frozen lake, bends dried cattails, and sends a blast of sharp crystals skyward. It's a three-hat day. I wear ear warmers, a wool cap, and a hood in addition to a vest, coat, mittens, and scarf—and I'm still cold on this fierce, grey morning. The skin on my face burns as I shoulder into the wind along the path leading to the stream. Snow that fell the night before fills the tops of my boots as I shuffle around iron-hard tussocks and sedges glistening with white beards. Not far off, the lake mutters in its icy bed. When I look out over crushed bulrush weighted down by snow, I can imagine the glaciers that carved this place.

Two million or more years ago, an ice age began in North America during the last part of the Pliocene Epoch, when a series of glacial invasions occurred from the far north. Slow-moving, massive sheets of ice and snow arranged and rearranged land forms like reckless, impatient pastry chefs pounding and kneading the earth. Glaciers are believed to have covered nearly one-third of the earth's land surface at the height of this glacial episode.

Glaciers pressed, pummeled, and scooped up new land forms, then melted and squashed hills and ridges flat again. As glaciers rumbled forward, they gathered up or crushed anything in their path—kneading boulders into cobbles, cobbles into gravel, gravel into sand. When glaciers wasted or melted, they spewed torrents of meltwater and dumped tons of soil, rocks, and debris. Hills, valleys, lakes, and rivers were destroyed, formed, and destroyed again. How many times? It's impossible to know for certain. I'm dizzied contemplating so much creation and destruction—all based on the whim of water and temperature.

The landscape I'm standing in was formed 25,000 to 14,000 years ago during the last gasps of the Pleistocene Epoch. The most recent sculpting of this part of Wisconsin by roving glaciers began when the Laurentide Ice Sheet stretched from present-day New York City west along what are now the Ohio and Missouri Rivers all the way to the Rocky Mountains. Nearly two-thirds of what we now know as Wisconsin was covered by ice and snow. This period was called the

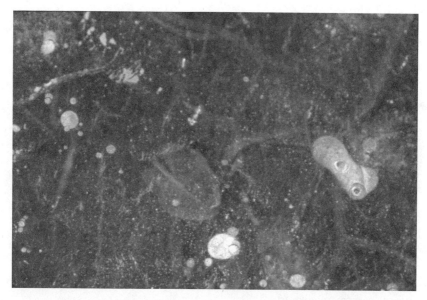

A clear layer of ice reveals last season's lilies, frozen bubbles, and glimpses of fish.

Wisconsin Glaciation because of the Wisconsin scientists who first identified and studied it.

No one knows for certain how many times glaciers may have rolled over this part of Wisconsin. Evidence of the Wisconsin Glaciation is most easily visible because it exists on top of evidence of earlier eras, which reveal themselves, according to one geologist, "like various ragged petticoats that droop out here and there around the skirt's hem or show in holes worn through upper layers."

The most recent glaciation moved south into Wisconsin like a six-fingered hand shoved into a too-small mitten. Each glacial lobe eased along at a different speed as the glacier ground south, then melted, then pushed forward again over a period of about 16,000 years.

Two adjacent lobes, the Green Bay and Lake Michigan Lobes, appear to have sideswiped and jammed against each other 14,000 to 16,000 years ago. The line of collision of these two in southeastern Wisconsin set the stage for the creation of this wetland and surrounding landscape.

I shut my eyes and try to picture how this terrain might have looked 25,000 years ago. It's a chilling thought; I would be buried beneath ice a mile thick. I shudder and wrap my scarf tighter around my neck. The icy grip of glaciers seems cataclysmic until I stop to consider that the ice age represents only a tiny fraction in the total boom-bust roller-coaster story of the Earth's life—less than one-tenth of a percent of known geologic time, which is estimated to be something like 5 billion years. By the time the ice age began, dinosaurs were long extinct and mammals that could withstand the cold were growing increasingly larger.

I've always found the ice age a terrifying concept. There's something awful about the notion that snow might fall and never melt, that spring might never come. As I hunker down into the biting wind, I can feel the biological tug of the Wisconsin Glaciation deep in my bones. The basic human dread that the fierce Midwestern winter might never end.

Why did the ice age begin? Scientists don't know for certain. Some point to massive shifts in climate caused by plate tectonic movement, the shift of continents. A few climatologists believe the ice age started when high-altitude westerlies in the Northern Hemisphere developed a bulge in their wind pattern that sent the westerlies careening far south over North America. As a result of shifting temperature patterns, vast areas of the world experienced a frigid zone of no summer.

Snow fell and never melted in the region north of what is now known as Hudson's Bay. Years and years passed and the snow compacted and became ice. The massive ice, driven forward by its own incredible weight and the effects of gravity, flowed outward like pancake batter poured on a griddle. Just as more batter would create more flow, more accumulated snow compressed and transformed into ice. The result? More glacial movement. Speeds may have ranged anywhere from a few inches to a few miles per year as the glaciers trundled along, sometimes colliding with each other, forming and reforming.

There were, geologists try to reassure us, periods of retreat, when the glaciers' vast frontal edges melted and appeared to pull back. "When conditions were bad they were terrible," writes Gwen

Schultz in *Ice Age Lost*. "But they weren't bad everywhere. They weren't bad all the time."

Meanwhile, I plunge my mittened hands deep into my pockets and glance downstream toward the frozen lake. In the distance I can hear the low moan and crack of the growing ice. The Green Bay and Lake Michigan Lobes must have been a thousand times noisier. From how many miles away was it possible to hear the roar and rumble of glaciers as they steamrolled through this part of Wisconsin?

Ice cracked and popped, stones rattled and grated. Every now and again the air filled with the sound of explosions as loud as gunfire as boulders split in half. The scraping and scudding must have been almost deafening as one glacier joined with another, shoving along surface debris that might include everything from clay, silt, sand and pebbles to boulders as big as automobiles and blocks of sedimentary rock as vast as football fields. Huge, dragged chunks of especially hard rock, such as granite, scraped and skidded and gouged the landscape. As they moved, glaciers polished rock surfaces with fine clay and sand.

Instead of cartoonish monoliths of smooth, pure white ice, I must imagine hulking, ever-changing mounds that jutted with cliffs and precipices as awry as bad teeth. Glaciers were often grubby-looking. Some were mottled blue and black. Others were streaked with red and brown dirt, striped with dramatic eye folds, or pocked with pink and yellow algae. Till, a combination of rocks and gravel, studded glaciers. Ice pinnacles crowned glaciers. It was not uncommon to find glaciers adorned with entire forests that had been ambushed along the way.

Each glacier was unique—a testament to constant change of temperature and terrain. Some glaciers' interiors were catacombed with tunnels and gushing waterways. In others, melting water trickled outward from surfaces riddled with holes. When ebbing streams froze at night as temperatures dropped, glaciers might have been wreathed in icicles.

Just as no glacier looked the same year after year, none rumbled forward or backward in a steady, predictable fashion. To say a glacier shifted gears and moved in reverse is an erroneous concept. What really happened was massive melting, what scientists describe as a retreat, an action more akin to watching a movie running backward.

When the climate warmed and a glacier thawed, its outward-most edge wasted or disappeared first. This part of the glacier was always the most unstable; like the youngest sibling in a big family, the outermost glacial edge was the unwilling victim of constant shoves from the larger, older body of ice.

Scientists don't know for certain when the Wisconsin Glacier began to retreat, or waste back. During a period of several thousand years, the ice melted, then moved forward, then melted again—a kind of push and pull. Schultz described the movement "like waves rolling onto a beach as the tide comes in. A wave rolls up and then falls back followed by another incoming wave which reaches up a little farther." Why did glaciers recede? One geologist wit replied, "to get more rocks."

Approximately 18,000 years ago, the Green Bay and Lake Michigan Lobes began to waste back and pull apart like the edges of an opening wound. The lobes' outermost borders receded farther and farther from each other. A thousand years passed. Then another. As the ice thawed and decayed, a nested series of partly collapsed outwash fans of gravel and debris was left behind, according to glacial geologist Lee Clayton of the Wisconsin Geological and National History Survey. These V-shaped mounds—looking almost like sculptures of open bird beaks—were not uniform, because of buried ice that created hummocks and low spots due to buried melting ice. What remains today is a ninety-mile-long ridge of knobby hills known as Kettle Moraine.

Slowly, the glaciers melted and shrank until what was left was the section of ice in protected snowy, cold retreats—the place where the glaciers were first formed. There was no exact calendar date when the ice age officially ended, although I have no trouble imagining what a marvel that moment might have been. The change was instead gradual and fluctuating and occurred over what would amount to hundreds and hundreds of human generations as shorelines moved and lake and ocean levels rose and fell.

What's remarkable is how long it took for geologists and historians to realize the glaciers' presence and effect both in Wisconsin and throughout the world. Not until the mid-nineteenth century did anyone begin to question or wonder whether something as enormous and powerful as a glacier might have changed the landscape so completely. Perhaps this is understandable. "When a glacier dies and drains away, nothing of itself remains," writes Schultz. "No crumpled ruin, no skeleton, no decayed residue. Where once loomed a robust traveling colossus thousands of feet high is only an emptiness of air."

Left behind was everything the glacier had been carrying: a carpet of rocks, sand, gravel, and boulders was strewn about in thin patches and layers as thick as a hundred feet. During warm weather, meltwater poured from the glacier and formed braided rivers and streams that flowed across the place where I am standing.

The landscape that had been transformed by frozen water was rearranged again—this time by running water. Milky rivers roared through the land, filled with rock flour, clay and silt that had been ground fine at the bottom of the glacier. Meltwater gurgled and rushed in spectacular torrents that flooded the lowland floor. A bird's-eye view of the unstable, ever-changing network of tangled channels would have revealed wild curves, islands, and knots of rock as flamboyant as the splash and dabble of a Jackson Pollock painting.

Icy currents shifted through the flat-bottomed valley and rumbled along the course of least resistance. When ice dams broke upstream, new tributaries spawned and connected. Blasts of water surged through deeper channels. Lake outlets shifted as floods filled depressions. Lakes suddenly emptied when dams of rock or ice were overwhelmed or melted away.

Meanwhile, the raging current sorted and redistributed tons of sand, gravel, and silt. Water scattered rocks that had been rounded like birds' eggs by the glacier. In some places outwash deposits buried the remnants of dead, or rotting, glacial ice. As this ice slowly melted over several centuries, it created steep-sided, water-filled hollows. Some of these hollows remained as lakes; others emptied slowly over time, leaving behind a steep-sided cavity later called a kettle.

Among other glacial-sculpted creations are drumlins, eskers, and kames. Drumlins have been described by one geologist as long hills shaped like overturned canoes; they are actually drag marks indicating what direction the glacier moved. Eskers are yet another kind of hill, long and winding and narrow. These were formed by meltwater *inside* glaciers. Over time sediments built up in the channels and tunnels. When the last ice was gone—voila! A new hill. Kames are small, cone-shaped hills created by a hole in the glacier through which debris-carrying water swirled and left an hour glass–bottom deposit on the uneven surface.

Left behind were discontinuous north-south trending moraines and ridges that look like rumples in the edge of a shoved-aside blanket. Every so often these ridges are punctuated by sags, water-filled hollows fed by the sluggish drainage system. Sand and gravel basins eventually became sealed with finer silts, causing water retention that would prove to be just right the depth for most semi-aquatic plants.

This lake and wetland may have been said to have celebrated their true birthday around 15,000 years ago. As glacial geologist Lee Clayton explained, until that point, "the lake had a long, obscure history." As I look out over the broad, flattened valley, I try to imagine the rushing water of meltwater rivers. The torrent of water dumped sand in depths of more than seventy feet in this area. More time passed. Some of the streams dried up. Others coursed along. Chunks of old ice buried deep underground melted slowly over many centuries. And this chaos of new hills, sand, and bulldozed beds of rocks and gravel helped create bad drainage—perfect conditions for creating a wetland.

Somehow it seems fitting on this freezing December morning to think that this wind-whipped, snow-covered lake had its genesis as a wayward chunk of ice from a dying glacier.

My husband and I trudge toward the stream where the canoe is overturned and discover that the ice in the stream has frozen clear. I walk out on to the stream and immediately feel dizzied by my height. In every other season except winter, I travel in the same place crouched in a kayak just above the water level. But now I feel enormous—upright and walking on top of the water. I gaze down into secret depths where an entire underwater landscape flourishes in spite of the cold. Stonewort, crisp pond weed, and coontail wave beneath the ice pushed by the current. Pieces of plants half-chewed, half-chopped—some just stems and buds blackened and mummified in the cold water—float past.

Warily, I walk along. How loud and heavy do my footsteps sound to any creature underneath the ice? Every so often the frozen stream reveals a porthole, a completely clear spot as big as the side of a hefty aquarium. I crouch and with my mitten rub away the dusting of snow and pinkish cattail fluff. Black creatures no bigger than my finger wriggle past. Another shape darts away in panic.

Sunlight can still filter through the ice into the lake's depths, where some pond plants continue to produce oxygen through photosynthesis. Because cold water absorbs and retains more oxygen than warm water, fish and aquatic insects with gills can survive here, "the one assured refuge from freezing," writes naturalist Bernd Heinrich in *Winter World.* And the ice provides a barrier from many predators.

Somewhere beneath my boots thrive the tadpoles of green frogs and bull-frogs and the larvae of caddis flies, stoneflies, and mayflies—not to mention diving beetles that hijack bubbles of air to continue breathing. Dragonfly eggs and larvae, so small that I can't see them, cling to underwater plant remains. Dragonfly larvae are underwater predators that have unique killer lips, hinged traps that sticks out from their heads. In a split second, with bristly lobes the larvae can snatch their prey.

While above the icy surface nothing moves except a snowy whirlwind, an entire universe flashes past below. I am mesmerized by these glimpses of the cold, watery world, and I wonder about everything I can't see. Somewhere buried underneath the mud are sleeping turtles and hibernating frogs.

Earlier in the fall, the resident snapping turtle, three feet long from tail to snout and weighing up to fifty pounds, buried itself underwater in stream bed mud to avoid predators. The turtle's breathing, movement, heart action appeared to cease as its resting metabolism dramatically dropped. A sleeping turtle has low oxygen needs because it does not move and its body temperature is kept so low. No one is sure exactly how the snapping turtle survives as it rests with its head and legs fully extended. Some scientists believe it may position itself in this way to take up through its skin as much dissolved oxygen as possible. Painted turtles bury themselves completely in the mud underwater near shore, perhaps because this is the place the water will warm up fastest with spring's return.

Snow falls among sedges along the icy water's edge.

Adult leopard frogs survive the winter buried in the mud at the bottom of the lake. If I could sit still long enough and watch the hibernating frogs, I'd see that they adjust their positions every so often. Leopard frogs can withstand cold water but cannot freeze solid like the tiny, one-inch-long spring peeper. In autumn the spring peeper crawls beneath leaf litter, logs, and tree roots in the woods surrounding the wetland. Its body creates a kind of glucose that serves as an anti-freeze which limits dehydration and protects cells from damage as the frog's body actually freezes solid.

As I peer into the depths, I'm startled by something brown and large that shoots under my feet. With amazing speed, a beaver or perhaps a muskrat barrels through the water and vanishes. Beavers have been known to swim like seals around and around in ponds in a clockwise course, according to one observer, "with no apparent objective in mind except to experience their own motility." While I shiver above the ice, the beaver with no enemies in sight may be enjoying exhilarating freedom of movement below.

When the lake freezes, muskrats feed on underwater roots of plants grubbed from the mud. A muskrat, protected by thick, waterproof fur and powered by partially webbed hind feet, can swim underwater for twelve minutes before it needs to come up for air. In winter the muskrat keeps open breathing holes in the ice by continuously poking its head up in certain spots as the ice is forming or by chewing through ice cracks. The muskrat plugs the breathing holes with dead vegetation that freezes in a clump—a kind of handy trap door—so that it can more easily come up for air and not be seen by soaring hawks or predators, such as coyotes, on land.

The muskrat needs a minimum of three inches of water beneath the ice in which to maneuver by burrowing through the mud. Any less, and it faces catastrophe: a freeze-out, which causes massive migration and likely death in the snow above ground.

I step closer to the stream's edge to try and examine a frowsy cattail flower head. Without warning, the ice gives way. GLUB! I sink hip-deep into icy water, and my boot touches something soft. Luckily, my one leg remains on what's left of the ice. Somehow I manage to hold my camera above my head.

I am so surprised, I can't believe I've fallen in. Fortunately, my husband pulls me to safety by hauling me out of the ice hole by my armpits. Even as he does this, my mind seems to protest. *Why are you helping me? I'm fine. I'm fine.*

Grateful but half-soggy, I trudge back up the path with one leg dry, one leg wet, my boot caked in glistening, black swamp mud. I hurry to try and get warm. Unlike a bird or mammal that falls into the icy depths by accident, I have a warm house to return to. Somehow I think I can hear muskrats laughing at me as I hurry past the last stand of cattails.

I still have much to learn.

# *January*

In winter the wetland holds its secrets dearly. To look for signs of life means to be ready, eyes open, ears and nose working. What seems like nothing might be something.

In winter, signs of life are subtle. I must stop, even though my teeth chatter, and stand perfectly still—watchful for a mouse, unwary and foolish, to dart out of a snow tunnel underneath the bent grass. There are clues everywhere, if I take the time to look. A pheasant's lost feather. Tiny sparrow footprints. The dodging, delicate hoof print of a doe pressed like an icy valentine into the path. The scattering of seeds by some nibbler. The scat of coyote right in the middle of the path. A kind of bold declaration, "I was here!"

From low gray clouds snow begins to fall. Fat flakes slant through the rattling dry sedges and cattail stems that stand taller than me. White fills the cold spaces between the red osier and clings to cattail seed heads and the stems of dry arrowroot and bulrush.

No birds chatter. Even the wind is hushed. Falling snow deadens sound in a peculiar way. I remain perfectly still and suddenly recall the dusty quiet of standing backstage in my father's theater enveloped in velvet curtains that seemed to stretch upward all the way to heaven. Here in the wetland, with snow covering my shoulders, my arms, my head, I can speak but no one can hear me. Words float only inches from my mouth and stop as if frozen. Snow makes me feel the same way I did inside the folds of that theater's ancient stage curtain: invisible and voiceless yet transported into another dimension.

Now the sun glimmers through milky sky. Snow sputters and stops.

Depth of snow during the winter can determine life or death for many creatures who make the wetland their home. An inch of new snow may mean starvation for a swamp sparrow that can't find fallen seeds. For a meadow mouse, an inch of snow may provide a life-saver—just enough cover to tunnel and safely escape from the sight of a prowling fox. When the snow cover is deeper, a grouse may find a hiding place by burrowing under the snow to sleep off the storm. Deep snow may further shield from predators the hibernating wood frog and chorus frog that hide under dead leaves, tree bark, and fallen branches and toads that hibernate underground in gopher mounds—just below the frost line.

Deeper yet, however, snow becomes a problem of survival for many mammals who frequent the wetland. While a fox can tread in half a foot of snow without too much difficulty, other animals, such as squirrels and rabbits, have to bound through the drifts and use up much more energy. Hungry white-tailed deer born late in the season can find haunch-high drifts of thirty inches or more a death sentence. Slowed by their lack of food, they are more easily hunted down by coyotes.

Deer seek out the shallower snow areas under spruces and evergreen at the edge of the wetland. This morning I find the trampled places under trees where deer rested out of sight during daylight hours. At sunset they look for food—pulling twigs and bark from birch, yew, and sumac. Around the wetland in winter are signs of hungry deer nibbling saplings down to the nub. Deer have eaten the buds off the branches of oak trees. Hemlock and cedar needles are their favorite winter food. While a rabbit uses its sharp front teeth and makes a clean cut of stem, a deer has to use its molars and leave behind a jagged cut where they've torn away a tender branch or bud.

In winter animals struggle to save energy in their movements. More motion requires more energy and, as a consequence, more food. Snow tracks tell stories. They reveal what was here, how fast it was moving, where it went, what it met—all clues I cannot find so easily any other time of the year. I follow the well-trampled trails of deer and discover the paw prints of the secretive red fox that frequents

A pair of coyotes leave their side-by-side tracks across new snow.

the brushy overgrowth near our barn. The fox's tracks are a study in careful efficiency. While the marks can often be confused with my Labrador Retrievers' tracks, a fox in winter seems to move much more sensibly. No rolling on its back and lunging crazily here and there like my dogs. A fox in midwinter is all business. Its tracks reveal a steady, careful, evenly spaced gait in a perfectly straight line. A successful hunt means survival.

The fox track closely follows the wood's edge or the slight ridge that runs along the wetland where a low wall once stood. Straight when traveling between areas, wandering when hunting, and circling when about to bed down—these are the signs of a fox. Always on the alert, the fox saves energy by walking in shallow snow, staying out of the wind, and resting where it can absorb maximum sun rays wherever possible. To survive on reduced prey that's often more difficult to catch, the nocturnal fox is known in winter to hunt during the day. I've never found a fox resting in midday, curled upon a protected spot, bush tail curled about it, napping for a few seconds at a time. I've found plenty of distinctive fox scat about: twisted, two to three-inches long, and pointed at one end.

## *February*

I trudge down the path toward the river. From a distance I catch a glimpse of the lake, which looks flat, slate-colored. The ice makes a moaning, sucking sound, like a bad toilet plunger or a deep bass plucked again and again. Sometimes I hear a kind of squawk, and I have to remind myself it is not a bird, it is the growing ice talking.

I glance through the binoculars at the other side of the lake. At the far end, where the water is still unfrozen, rests a family of mute swans—five cygnets, or babies, plus their parents. This is the biggest swan family I've seen yet to survive together. Their pale bodies, all the same size now, blend into the snow that surrounds a patch of rapidly shrinking open water. A family of mallards, who would ordinarily not dare come so close to these large, fiercely territorial birds, shares space with the bad-tempered swans. Winter has a way of forcing companionship among even the most incompatible.

Beyond the open water, up the inlet, is the home of a particularly crowded winter housing arrangement. It is the large den of beavers. The last time I visited the beaver's growing lodge, there were nearly two feet of new gnawed branches and chewed sticks piled atop it. The lodge has a chamber inside with two underwater entrances. Now even the mud on the top of the lodge is frozen hard and snow-covered. Yet, inside the temperature may be 34 degrees Fahrenheit even when it's as cold as 30 below outside.

Living inside the cramped, dark lodge may be as many as six beavers: two adults, two or more yearlings, and two or more kits born in last spring. Unlike the swans, the beavers sleep during most of the winter to conserve energy. It's a crowded—but warm—arrangement.

Outside the lodge I've seen the pile of saplings that the beavers cut and stacked in the fall. They drag these to their feeding platform, a special level inside the lodge, and strip away the softer wood and bark to eat. This action helps wear down their teeth, which will grow out of control if they don't use them in this way. In late fall I often saw fat beavers lolling along the water's edge, stuffing themselves until they looked as if they might burst. This time of year it would be unusual to find a beaver's tracks in the snow—even as evidence that a beaver had been snacking.

If beavers wake up hungry, they know better than to wander aboveground exposed to their enemies in such cold. They have a handy winter travel strategy: they exit from the lodge into the water under the ice and swim until they find a breathing space poked through the ice by a muskrat. Walking on the surface of the frozen lake, I have occasionally come upon beaver bubbles, globules of trapped air expelled from beavers' lungs as they swim. The dancing air bubbles, according to some beaver experts, are a sure sign that the beaver colony is wintering successfully.

As I walk along the icy path, wind grates and rubs the dried cat-tail stalks together. The noise sounds like an old man rubbing his hands together. *Whoosh, whoosh, whoosh.* I try to listen for the sound of a muskrat's desperate chewing. In the cold, I cannot tell the differ-ence between muskrat munching and the rustling of dead stalks.

Standing here, it's hard for me to believe that cattail roots still thrive beneath the stranglehold of ice. The starchy root stocks form a thick mat beneath the water—now a frozen shield. The hollow stems break like straws in my hands. The cattail seed heads remain a kind of study in patience, hope, and abundance. Velvet, dark brown seed heads bob and sway in the wind. When my young nephew first saw them, he demanded, "Who put the hot dogs on the sticks?"

If I pick one of the seed heads and rub the soft surface with my thumb, the seed head quickly falls apart into a handful of pinkish fluff that looks like stuffing from a dilapidated couch cushion. Each starry-shaped fluff carries one tiny brown cattail seed—light enough to be sent airborne by a puff of wind. Amazingly, each cattail seed head is packed with 125,000 seeds. Cattail fluff makes excellent insulation for mice nests and, later, a soft lining of bird's nests. The intact seed head is also a perfect hideout. Deep inside this tightly packed seed head may be cattail moth larvae. In the fall, invading larvae took the extra precaution of spinning silk around the cattail head to help keep it from blowing away. If all goes well, the larvae will hibernate until spring, when flocks of noisy, jostling red-winged blackbirds arrive and land in and knock about the cattails—helping to liberate the larvae.

When dead cattail stalks fall to the ground, they decompose and become soil. The cattails' success would seem to spell its own demise. The more cattails, the more land. The more land, the less wet land. And since cattails can only support themselves in soggy places, it would seem that their very success guarantees their future doom.

Enter our hero, the muskrat.

The ranging, ever hungry, ever prolific wetland mammal has a special relationship with cattails. All parts of the cattail serve the muskrat's needs. In winter the muskrat digs up and eats cattail roots. Dried and fresh stems serve as perfect building material for muskrat lodges. When spring returns and the first stems and leaves appear, the muskrats will dine on these with gusto.

As I stand in the dried cattails, I can see the muskrat trails twist and turn through the wetland. In the die-back it's easy to spot the muskrat's snow-covered routes. There's little neat Midwestern geometry in the tracks—no clean grid of east and west, north and south axis. No, the muskrat is a meanderer. I follow a wandering, wayward muskrat trail and quickly discover that the route has been recently used as a highway by mice that have left their tiny tracks out in the open—making them easy targets for flying hawks.

Muskrat highways head directly from the stream to thick stands of cattails. How long have these routes been here? How many generations of muskrats have scurried along these same byways? When summer comes, I know I will not be able to see these passages. As cattails send up new shoots and the growth of rushes pulses and thickens, the trails will again become invisible. Secret exits and entrances will become hidden.

## Trickster in Winter

More than two centuries ago, members of the Wisconsin Ho-Chunk Nation may have lived near this wetland. One of their early myths concerned Trickster, also called *wakdjunkaga,* which means "the tricky one." Anthropologist Paul Radin (1883–1959) studied the Wisconsin tribe extensively. He described Trickster as "at one and the same time creator and destroyer, giver and negator, he who dupes others and who is always duped himself." The Trickster possesses no values, moral or social, is at the mercy of his passions and appetites, yet through his actions, Radin says, all values come into being. He is sometimes identified with different animals—such as the coyote, raven, hare, and spider. But in the Ho-Chunk story, he has no form. He is an "inchoate being of undetermined proportions, a figure foreshadowing the shape of man."

The Trickster myth cycle was passed along in the form of stories handed down by word of mouth from generation to generation. The tales are filled with humor and a very earthy irony. It's easy to imagine groups of Ho-Chunk sitting around a fire in the dead of winter listening to Trickster's adventures and laughing. Trickster is ourselves, he is a celebration of the ambiguity of all humans trying to figure out our world. Many of the creatures that play a part in Trickster's adventures are wetland dwellers: mink, muskrat, beaver, hawk, snipe, duck, and turtle—to name a few.

## Trickster Visits the Muskrats in Winter

Winter was very long, and Trickster and his wife and children had no food. So Trickster decided to visit the village of the muskrats. All the muskrats cheered when they saw him coming, which made Trickster feel very happy. Even the muskrat children chanted, "Our uncle has come! Our uncle has come!"

Old Muskrat welcomed Trickster into his lodge. "Old woman," he told his wife, "my older brother has come. Prepare some food right away. Boil him some roots of the lily-of-the-lake."

So the old wife handed Old Muskrat a pail and a sharp awl and he took these and went out on to the frozen lake. He came back with ice in the pail. Old muskrat took the sharp awl and chipped away at the ice, "POCK, POCK, POCK."

Old Muskrat Wife took the pail with the ice and hung it from a hook over the fire. To Trickster's amazement, in a short while she dished out some lily-of-the-lake roots, which were very delicious. Trickster ate and ate until his belly bulged.

"You seem very hungry, Uncle," said Old Muskrat, who was always very polite. "Would you like to take some lily-of-the-lake roots with you for your wife and children?"

Trickster, who was very proud but very cunning, shook his head. "No, no, my younger brother. We have something to eat at our house, too," Trickster lied.

When it was time for Trickster to leave, he purposefully left one of his mittens under Old Muskrat's lodge mat. "Goodbye, younger brother," Trickster said. But when he'd walked away a few feet, he shouted back, "Say, younger brother! I left one of my mittens at your house. Let one of the children bring it over to me."

Old Muskrat knew that Trickster might be up to something. So he warned his children, "Take this mitten over to your uncle. But remember: he always talks a good deal. Go only part of the way and throw it at him."

The muskrat child took Trickster's mitten and did as he was told. "Here, Uncle!" But just as he was about to throw the mitten, Trickster called out in his most friendly manner.

"Come a little closer!" Trickster said. "Come over to me with the mitten. I dread going back because I am so old."

So the muskrat child, being obedient, did as he was told. "Tell your father that in the morning," Trickster told the muskrat child, "he is to come and see me."

When the muskrat child returned to his parents' lodge, he told his father what Trickster had said.

Old Muskrat groaned. "I knew he would say something like that, and that is why I asked you to throw the mitten at him."

"Well," explained the muskrat child, "I did go part of the way and wanted to throw it at him but he told me not to, that he dreaded to go back over the ice."

So the next day, Old Muskrat paid a visit to Trickster and his wife and children. It would have been very rude to bring along any food, so he came empty handed.

"Welcome, younger brother!" said Trickster. "I can't believe you came on such a blustery, cold day, but here you are. Well, younger brother, what do you want to eat? Old woman," Trickster called to his wife, "give me my bag and my sharp instrument."

Trickster's wife was embarrassed but she did as she was told. What was Trickster up to this time?

Trickster went to the ice and whacked away at it for quite a while. "POCK, POCK, POCK, POCK, POCK." He filled his bag with so much ice he could hardly drag it back to his lodge. Trickster put a kettle on the fire and poured ice into it.

Trickster's wife watched with alarm. Her husband seldom cooked. "Brother-in-law," she murmured with great shame to Old Muskrat, "I do not know why my husband is acting so odd. He must have seen you do something."

The kettle boiled and steamed and soon there was so much bubbling that the water hissed and overflowed and put out the fire. Trickster's children whimpered with hunger as they watched their father dump the kettle out empty outside the lodge.

Trickster scratched his head. "I wonder why the kettle acted in this strange way? I've always been able to cook this recipe before."

Old Muskrat looked at Trickster's skinny children and his shame-faced wife. Old Muskrat sighed and took Trickster's bag. He went out on to the frozen lake and came back with a heavy bag. He brought it back full of ice and poured the contents out on the side of Trickster's lodge. The ice turned into lily-of-the-lake roots. Trickster's children cheered. Old Muskrat went back again with the bag and again came back with a heavy load of lily-of-the-lake roots. Four times he did this.

"Thank you, thank you, Old Muskrat!" said Trickster's wife.

Trickster turned to his wife angrily and said, "You wicked old woman, what are you saying? How often have I done this for you, yet you never thanked me for it! Yet you thank Old Muskrat!"

Old Muskrat did not want to get in the middle of their argument, so he went home to his own lodge.

With satisfaction Trickster inspected the great mountain of lily-of-the-lake roots. "Old wife," he said, "this is the way you are supposed to act in order to have plenty of lily-of-the-lake roots, so muskrat told me. At any rate, old woman, this ought to keep our bellies fed for some time. We will indeed have food for many days to come."

(Adapted from "Winnebago Trickster Cycle, Number 41" from *The Trickster: A Study in American Indian Mythology* by Paul Radin [New York: Schocken, 1956], 41–42.)

# Spring

The water stored in narrow pools escapes
In rivulets; the cold roots stir below.
Theodore Roethke,
"The Light Comes Brighter"

# ℳarch

Water purls beneath shrinking drifts. Snow melt gurgles, trickles, glistens, and glitters in the bright sunlight. Wherever a stalk or shoot or stem stands upright, a neat cavity has been formed around the base. Each plant, however brittle and dead-looking, gives off enough heat to create a kind of collar in the snow.

With the sun shining and the sky bright blue, winter—now that it's nearly gone—looks benign. It's the same way we feel when we're almost recovered from a terrible illness. We look back, weary, haggard, yet we think to ourselves, "Oh, that wasn't really so bad." Of course that thought would never have crossed our minds while we were in the midst of our suffering and there seemed to be no end in sight.

Had all creatures known what was coming, what heady, exhilaration they must have felt during the last days of the ice age, the ablation season, as it's been called. The Great Melt. Every year I feel a sense of exquisite relief at even the hint that winter might release its iron grip. How much more exhilarating would spring seem if winter lasted thousands of years?

Of course no bell gonged, no calendar page turned to mark the end of the ice age. No one probably guessed the ice age was ending. How could they? No one lived long enough to tell the difference. If time-lapse photography from a satellite directed at Wisconsin had been possible 18,000 years ago, the great ice sheets would have looked like "active amoebas," according to scientist E. C. Pielou, "with undulating outlines, wobbling unsteadily as they contracted to nothing."

When the ice finally disappeared what remained was an unpromising looking landscape strewn with boulders, gravel, and heaps of sand and littered with innumerable glacial puddles, icy lakes, and cold, sediment-choked rivers. Glacial till—the refuse of glaciers—is a Scottish term that means "stiff, indurated stony ground." Even the definition has a perfect inhospitable, uncompromising ring to it.

The climate, too, was anything but gentle. During late spring and summer the air remained cold and clammy. Most of the ground was still imprisoned in a layer of permafrost. The place where I stand was open, treeless. Wind howled and buffeted clouds of dust. To the north there was nothing—not a tree in sight—to slow the blast of air from the arctic.

And yet, in spite conditions that seemed too cold, too rocky, too uninhabitable, something amazing happened.

Plants grew.

Wind helped transform the landscape. Soil and seeds that existed to the south—beyond the reach of the glacier's grip—were picked up by wayward gusts and dumped into the flat expanse of "deranged drainage," a chaotic array of small basins still not efficiently connected. Little by little, lichens and mosses sprouted and held tight to bare rocky outcrops and sparse particles of windblown soil. A stubborn mat of tiny, crude plants erupted from between the cracks of rocks. These first hardy pioneer plants—lichens resembling ruffled mats and others that cling to rocks like flaky paint—are the same kind found in tundras and on mountains with elevations as high as 18,000 feet above sea level. In time, as lichens and mosses died and sprouted and died, the first layers of organic material built up and allowed other vegetation to get started.

Approximately 14,000 years ago, tundra-tolerant plants such as saxifrage and bright yellow arctic poppy, arctic willow and grasses, and purple broad-leafed willow herb grew in fuzzy, compact clumps nestled among remaining heaps of rocks. These plants hugged the ground to avoid being dried out by the ever-present wind. They could withstand unexpected freeze-ups and grow nestled under insulating layers of snow. Dark leaves provided better heat absorption. To take advantage of every available sunny day, they budded and flowered early.

As tundra plants died and decomposed, they in turn became part of an organic mat that set the stage for other plants. Eventually, seeds of shrub willow, juniper, buffalo berry, and wolf willow took hold. As the permafrost released its stranglehold, scraggly stands of trees began to appear. Black spruce with branches like bottle brushes were among the first trees to creep into southeastern Wisconsin from the south. White spruce, which can withstand extremely low temperatures and heavy snow, was another pioneer tree. The tightly wound waxy needles of the white spruce held in moisture and prevented death in strong winter winds. Juniper, ash, and a few aspen began to dot the landscape. There were no true forests yet—just small stands of desperate, wind-blasted trees.

Out in the lake the establishment of the earliest aquatic plants required more time to develop. The first important step was for the water to clear enough for sunlight to penetrate and warm the deepest reaches. Years passed before the cold, ice-fed lake bottom thickened with enough sediment to support plants, which in turn created rich organic material to support *more* plants, such as slender naiad, broad-leafed arrowhead, cattails, sedges, and burr reeds.

With the arrival of plants in and around the lake and streams came animals and hordes of insects. Mosquitoes, midges, flies, and dragonflies arrived, followed by insect-eating birds, which in turn carried such mollusks as tadpole snails. Once the murky rivers and lakes settled and cleared, mollusks, algae, diatoms, and primitive fish called killifish were among the first arrivals. Some fish were swept into the glacial landscape from other places. Immature mussels arrived as hoboes, attached to fish.

According to fossil records, what's now known as the Eastern American toad was probably one of the first amphibians to make this wetland its home. Hardy and thick-skinned, the toad withstands subzero temperatures by burying itself in the ground and hibernating. By holding perfectly still, its chunky, earth-colored body provides excellent camouflage. Another early arrival was the hardy wood frog, which can freeze solid in winter, thanks to the anti-freeze–like chemicals in its blood.

Mammals such as shrews, rabbits, and meadow vole were pioneering species along with beaver, porcupine, and river otter. Large mammals included black bear and moose. All of these were followed by predators such as coyotes, foxes, and grey wolves.

There was no steady, orderly march of animals and plants into the area once scoured by glaciers. Patchwork settlements of pioneer species appeared in a kind of mosaic. Those better adapted to survive the cold held stolidly to more northerly ranges. Those who could not stand the shift died or moved. Of all the pioneering species, birds such as mallards, northern shovelers, Canada geese, and ravens could fly away to more hospitable climates with the most ease.

The wetland resounds with the twangy banjo calls of green frogs like this one.

Fossils for all of these types of birds have been found dating back to the Wisconsin Glaciation.

Plants and animal communities are always in disequilibrium, writes biologist Margaret Davis. "[They're] continually adjusting to climate and continually lagging behind and failing to achieve disequilibrium before the onset of a new climatic trend." In other words, the living world is not marvelously attuned to the environment but is instead always trying to catch up and adapt, never quite succeeding, because climate changes continuously. Vegetation never catches up. Neither do we. Somehow, instead of finding this idea disheartening, I find it hopeful. Perhaps because what may appear a dispiriting situation always has the potential for transforming into something completely different.

Between 12,500 and 10,000 years ago, coniferous forests of black and white spruce took hold in the hills and around the edges of the wetland and fen. Grasslands developed. New invaders into the landscape included a host of frogs: spring peeper, striped chorus frog, pickerel frog, mink frog, grey tree frog. Fossil bone records show that the green frog was an early invader, as well as the cold-tolerant painted turtle, soft-shell turtle, and Blanding's turtle. Enter the first snakes: the northern water snake and the common garter snake and the first salamanders, the blue-spotted salamander.

The white spruce, with its four-sided needles and bark covered with sticky gum, was a favorite food of mastodons, one of a host of megaherbivores that probably visited this wetland. About 11,000 years ago, the enormous shaggy mastodons standing ten feet at the shoulder with outward curving tusks wandered into this part of Wisconsin to munch on willows and spruce trees and drink water from the streams and lakes by sucking water up through their long trunks and spraying it into their mouths.

Equally enormous were the woolly mammoths, which had high-domed skulls, smaller ears, and shorter trunks than mastodons. The woolly mammoth's tusks were so huge they were often twisted inward. Frozen woolly mammoth carcasses discovered in Siberia have revealed that the creatures had long, shaggy ginger-colored coats to withstand fierce winter blasts. The woolly mammoth preferred to eat grass and small shrubby plants and frequently fell victim to snow-covered bogs. While strolling across the bogs, the giant creatures were often trapped in the mud and died. Woolly mammoth molars with surfaces as rough as washboards and mastodon leg bones have been found in what was once a marsh only a few miles from here. Other evidence of large wetland visitors include antlers from giant elk, which were discovered in a stream bed. A male giant elk stood five feet at the shoulder and weighed as much as nine hundred pounds.

Herds of grazing barren-ground or tundra caribou, weighing two hundred to four hundred pounds, had distinctive backward curling antlers. Flat-headed peccaries, which bore striking resemblance to wild boars, roved in brawling packs. Their sharp, protruding lower teeth were used to fight or dig for roots in wet meadows. Giant beaver nearly as big as black bears clumsily roved marshes in search of aquatic life to eat. These animals were considered the largest rodent the world has ever known. Unlike the modern beaver, the giant had a round tail, incisor-like teeth, and not much in the way of brains.

# Spring

As I scan the wetland on a bright, spring morning, I wonder about the first humans who came here to hunt and camp. Who were they? Where did they come from? No one knows for certain.

Nearly 50,000 years ago humans may have first migrated to North America from Asia following herds of bison and other game across a land bridge near Siberia. Among radiocarbon dated clues found in what's now northern Alaska are butchered bones from meals and evidence that dogs had already been domesticated. Scientists believe that at the end of the ice age, between 12,000 and 9,000 years ago, early human residents were already established in what's now Wisconsin and the Great Lakes Basin.

Because these Paleoindian hunting bands must have had to travel quickly on foot to follow herds of game, they probably had few possessions they took with them. There are no written records about their lives. They left behind no pottery, no evidence of gardens, no bows and arrows. Few pieces of cave art survive. What we have as their record are weapons and tools made of weather-proof stone. Distinctive, leaf-shaped fluted points, or spear heads, must have been painstakingly chipped from stone. These are called fluted points because they have a flute or groove down the middle of both sides. Scientists believe that this acted like the groove on a bayonet and promoted bleeding to weaken large game. The wooden shaft of the spear was notched. The end of the shaft was where the point was bound with twine-like sinew. Other tools that have been discovered include: stone hide-scrapers, stone knives, small pointed tools called gravers, which were used to poke a hole in hide.

Paleoindians may have sojourned near this wetland—a perfect place to hunt, fish, and gather plants or berries. Three folsom points, fluted points named for their shape, were found 20 miles away near the outlet of Lake Delevan. Two of the points were made of Burlington chert, the other was of Moline chert. Chert is a dull-colored, flint-like quartz found in Iowa and Illinois, showing that Paleoindians traveled and traded.

Naturally, early spear points are hard to find. If it took an individual many hours to create one point, it's doubtful that the weapon point would be thrown away after a kill. Most likely these weapons were pulled out to be reused. Likewise, we have little evidence of Paleoindian housing. Did they make shelters from brush or did they sleep in caves? Scientists assume they traveled in small family groups. What they left behind were fire-blackened bones and bones butchered with distinctive cuts. Some bones were broken so that marrow could have been consumed. Paleoindians frequently removed from a kill site certain mastodon bones that are believed to have been used for stripping hides.

The most abundant and accessible food for Paleoindian hunters was terrestrial animals that roamed around the area nibbling on cattails, sedges, willows, and stands of spruce. While they lasted, these game animals included the mammoth, mastodon, caribou, moose, elk, and bear. Other smaller wetland game were white tail deer, rabbits, squirrels, muskrats, and turtles.

Woolly mammoths became extinct in Wisconsin 12,400 years ago. The mastodons managed to hang on another thousand years or so browsing in mixed conifer-hardwood forests. The entry of Paleoindian hunters on the scene and the extinction of so many large herbivores shortly thereafter has long fascinated scientists. Did these early hunters cause a massive overkill? It's hard to imagine, since humans' only weapons were long spears and a group effort to flush out game with fire. Animals may have stampeded toward a bog or wetland, where they became mired and trapped, easy targets for the final kill.

Mysteriously, at the close of the Wisconsin Glaciation, not only the mastodon and mammoth but also the giant beaver and giant elk became extinct. In just one thousand years in the Great Lakes region, the short-faced bear, giant beaver, flat-headed peccary, and woodland musk ox also vanished. No one is certain exactly why. Of the thirty large mammals in the Great Lakes area, 63.333 percent became extinct. Only 3.33 percent of the sixty-one small mammals suffered the same fate. Somehow, the smaller animals with higher reproductive rates and less demanding appetites may have had a better chance surviving.

Theories abound about the giant herbivore die-off. Some believe that mastodons weakened as climate changed and available plants shifted from spruce forest, which mastodons preferred, to a mixed forest dominated by oak trees. In less than a human lifetime, spruce disappeared from the area. Other scientists point to the fact that the woolly mammoth and mastodon needed salt and were unable to find this essential nutrient in salt licks during a climate shift that caused drought conditions. Hotter summers and colder winters meant that woolly mammoth and mastodon offspring may have had trouble surviving. Other scientists theorize that new diseases brought by migrating animals across the Bering Strait may have infected and killed off the megaherbivores. The answer is probably a combination of all these factors.

What is clear, however, is that in the course of several human lifetimes, the large herbivores began to dwindle and then vanish. "It is tempting to speculate," writes scientist E. C. Pielou in *After the Ice Age,* "on how many generations of human children marveled at stories of their forefathers' mammoth-hunting exploits and of their encounters with sabertooths."

Somewhere out in the wetland, buried deep in the mud and muck, may be the bones of one of the many hapless woolly mammoths or mastodons that once roamed here. In 1964 a farmer in Kenosha County, about fifty miles from here, decided to drain a wetland to increase his plowed acreage. While digging the tile line that would be used to drain away water, the farmer discovered the remains of a skeleton. He called archaeologists, who identified the remains of a woolly mammoth that appeared to have been submerged in what was once a glacial lake after it was butchered. The bones, which had been neatly piled by sizes, featured telltale butcher marks made only by humans. Another clue of human presence was that the mammoth's mandible, or jaw bone, was missing—a common occurrence wherever humans did butchering. Discovery of the remains of a two-sided tool called a biface convinced scientists to do radiocarbon dating of the bone collagen. They found that the site dated back 10,000 to 12,480 years.

At the Kenosha Public Museum the woolly mammoth skeleton has been carefully reassembled. The bones, so carefully preserved in lake clay and peat of the marsh, now bear a striking resemblance to what Irish poet Seamus Heaney called, in a poem describing an elk skeleton preserved in a bog and later reassembled, "an astounding crate full of air." Like Heaney and his giant Irish elk, I wonder where this mammoth traveled and what wetland plants it feasted on before it died.

## Constant Transformation

Returning geese call overhead at sunset. They sound like a high school marching band practice breaking up. The brass section gives one last oomph and squawk. Between dying notes, flaps of feathers, rush of raw wind.

As soon as the snow and ice begin to thaw, Canada geese are among the first migrating waterfowl to head north. They make the journey from warmer climates in southern Illinois and Kentucky to breeding grounds in Hudson's Bay. Canada flocks average about a hundred birds. Geese travel in V-formation, which cuts wind resistance and makes flying easier for the group. The lead bird is usually a gander, or male goose. Under low, heavy, overcast skies, the flock may fly only a few hundred feet above the ground. With fair skies, geese have been recorded at altitudes of more than 8,000 feet. Wetlands along their journey provide welcome rest stops.

As darkness descends, I sniff the air. Something smells different. A faint softness—the scent of damp earth and promise of returning light, new growth.

That night snow falls again. The next morning new snow has filled the trail, sheathing brittle cattails, bright red osier branches, and ghostly, rattling bulrush stems. It's so cold I can see my breath.

On my way out to the swamp still amid the tangle of shrubs I hear a call as faint as the zithering clink of a metal zipper. I look carefully for movement. There among the dead branches and dangling leaves are a half dozen juncos. Their white feathers, dipped black bodies conceal tiny beating hearts, bright eyes. Clinging to stalks, they resemble dried seed pods swinging in the wind. Their tails are what make them unmistakable. As they fly away, their gray tails are lined on either side with white feathers. All winter the junco makes a twittering sound. Only in the earliest moments of spring, as the birds begin to leave the wetland and head north, can I hear the junco's high sustained trill—a new song that means it's time to migrate.

When I reach the stream's edge, I walk out as far as I dare, still avoiding the rotten ice in the middle. Water bubbles up through cracks in the ice. The brittle frozen edge shatters like glass under my heel. Up and down the water way ice sinks in chunks and sheets. What was captured below the frozen surface is now freed. The pale bloated body of a fish, a turtle's shell—remnants of animals that did not survive the winter in hibernation deep in the stream bed's soft mud. A hungry sea gull shrieks above the lake and dives for the dead fish.

Downstream two geese waddle side by side on the ice. They stroll along and squawk at each other like old friends. Returning snow and lingering ice do not seem to bother them. I, too, try not to feel discouraged by the slowness of spring in arriving.

I trail the edge of the water where the dry, sedgy tussocks stand bunched. They promise something solid underfoot. Beyond, I can see the drift of dark, open water where the current runs free. Pieces of purplish ice and dried bulrush bob and sweep past. The thick ice edge curls like a white lip against the licking water. While I watch, a section of ice as big as a tea tray slices free and pulls away almost as if it were powered by a motor. The stream appears to move faster than I remember it in warmer seasons.

Everything seems astir now—thawing by day, freezing by night. A constant transformation from solid to liquid, from liquid to solid. As I stand here watching the ice chunk float away, I have a vision of myself marooned on an iceberg like an unsuspecting polar bear adrift in an arctic sea. I step back.

Another piece cracks as neatly as if cut by a knife. I gaze through the camera—eager for a picturesque shot—and notice a scraggly patch of long grey fur stuck to the ice edge. The telltale sign of a possum's last struggle. Whose feast? I cannot tell. A coyote, perhaps. And I wonder if the diner was the coyote I heard the night before— the high, wide, crooning call of a male advertising his location.

Coyotes begin mating between February and March. While many pairs breed for many years in a row, they don't mate for life. Somewhere on the edge of the marsh, perhaps in an old, abandoned badger den, the coyote and its mate may dig a new den. I have often found such holes under upturned stumps. The entrance is ten inches wide and maybe a foot high. The coyote is a tidy housekeeper, unlike the careless fox that tosses bones and other debris about its yard. Foresight seems part of the coyote mother's nature. She digs two dens—just in case she and her brood of five to seven pups need to make a quick exit and find a new place to live.

Some time in April coyote pups will be born with short, yellow-brown fur and blind eyes. They cannot see until they are ten days old and begin to crawl around the den. The pups are fed by their father, who hunts for food. The pups remain in the den with their mother for about two months after their birth. By the time they are three weeks of age, they tumble out of the den and play. They're taught to hunt by their parents, and by the end of the summer, they move out of their parents' territory or sometimes join their parents and form a hunting pack.

Last fall I saw a cocky, grey coyote lope with long, thin legs through the scrubby brush on the marsh edge. As he trotted through the trees, he carried his black-tipped bushy tail low—unlike a wolf, who runs with his tail up and blazing. The inside of the coyote's ears, the edges of his mouth and throat were white. His eyes were yellow. Although he was probably only about forty pounds, he seemed much bigger. For a moment he paused, swiveled his large, pointed ears, and glared at me, as if to say, "I have been here long before you."

Coyotes mark their territories with urine, feces, and glandular scents that drive my dogs wild. Crafty and adaptable, coyotes thrive along the edge of the marsh as both scavenger and predator. There's plenty to eat. Any kind of meal will do for a coyote—possum, rabbit, mouse, fish, turtle—fresh or road-killed. Coyotes feast on berries on bushes or in my neighbor's corn field. They've been known to hunt down deer—but it's hardly worth the effort when a lazy possum can be killed. Coyotes gallop at a surprising average running speed of twenty-five miles per hour.

As I return from the stream through the marsh, I discover that the coyotes have left their story of last night in the snow. Pressed in the snow is a pair of footprints the size of a dog's, indicating that two coyotes were walking together and then single-file through the musk-rat trails. The new pair—perhaps male and female—clearly were not running. Their careful footprints reveal a steady walk. Their tracks crisscross the nervous, jittering trails of mice that appear to have fled into the cattails with tails dragging. The coyotes' tracks intersect the three-toed saunter of a ring-necked pheasant. A pheasant would have made an excellent dinner for a pair of hungry coyotes.

In winter ring-tailed pheasants resplendent in shimmering blue and green feathers huddle in the cattails in flocks of four to as many as 100. It's a harem affair, three female pheasants for every male. As soon as spring comes in earnest and the ground thaws and turns muddy, the pheasants will no longer be able to make their way with ease and they will leave the wetland. Right now the cattails provide a handy place to rest between meals in my neighbor's corn field.

Pheasants are an exotic immigrant to Wisconsin wetlands and fields. The first pheasants came to Milwaukee in a cage from China in 1893. There were eight of them, and they cost their owner five dollars a piece. The exotic "Mongolian" pheasants, as they were called, grew in number in spite of the harsh Wisconsin winters. The Milwaukee breeder's plan was to "liberate" the pheasants for hunting. Forty of his pheasants appeared to have had other ideas. They made an unplanned jailbreak and headed for the wilds of Waukesha County. The pheasant whose tracks I follow may have had ancestors among those early escape artists.

My trail is intertwined with the deep, explosive prints of a bounding rabbit. The coyote tracks swerve off to the south—perhaps in pursuit. But the pheasant's trail appears to amble away. There's no telltale sign of struggle, no bloody feathers or rumpled snow. I have no way to know for sure who may have escaped the coyote pair and who was eaten.

### First Arrivals

In the morning early before the sun rises high enough to burn off the new film of thin ice, the sedge-matted ground is stiff and strangely pliable. It makes a crunchy sound and creaks with each foot fall. The water beneath oozes and moans if I jump. Ground quivers. Puddles slosh. It feels as if I'm walking on a rotten roof—dry curled shingles, sagging boards. What exhilaration to dare to walk farther! See how far out I can go?

I am still standing.

Still.

I forgot the pleasure of walking on rotten ice. One foot placed on a completely untouched frozen clump and melting snow surrounding a tussock of matted grass and reed that suddenly gives way with a satisfying THUNK. My boot shifts lower, makes a squelching noise, and is quickly covered with cold water. I take another step. THUNK. It is the same delightful feeling of accomplishment of cracking a chocolate bar on the edge of a table or popping plastic bubble packing or chucking rocks at windows of an abandoned house.

Out on the marsh the first male red-winged black birds announce their return with their boastful call: KO KLA REE KO KLA REE. Once companionable flock mates, the red-winged males now seem to view each other with a surprising fierceness. KO KLA REE KO KLA REE. They land atop bobbing cattail heads. They swoop from birch branch to topmost cedar bough, trying to stake out territory. With every landing, these Romeos jostle and flare their bright red wing patches—a display they make for the benefit of all the other males that came with them in their migrating flock. There's not a female in sight yet, but their aggressive land grab has already begun.

Across the marsh the first arrivals of mated pairs of sandhill cranes clatter with a rising crescendo. GARROOO GARROOO-AAAAAH. The pairs' special unison calls echo back and forth from hidden spots among matted tussocks and bent reeds where they declare their nesting territory. Unlike red-wings, sandhills mate for life. In their nesting duet, the sandhill male raises his head straight up and calls. The female, who stands beside him and throws her head back about forty-five degrees, answers him in a shrill double echo. Back and forth they bugle. Every so often they may leap into the air, as if dancing.

Fossil records show that cranes have existed on earth for nearly 60 million years, making them one of the oldest living bird species. Cranes were ancient even before the glaciers rolled through this part of the region.

The songsters fill me with hope. I look up. Four groups of thirty or forty cranes soar in a steady V-formation from the south. They're moving northwest. As they fly high overhead, they make a low, purring noise, a kind of guttural acknowledgement. Always following the formation are one or two stragglers that send out a louder, desperate bugling as they flap and flap in attempt to catch up with the rest of the flock. This loose confederation of families may have wintered in Florida and are now seeking out spring nesting grounds in Wisconsin's wetlands.

Each time a group passes overhead, the sandhills hidden in the cattails around me let out a great cry as if to say: "Keep going! This spot is taken."

Watching and listening to the sandhills helps me imagine some other winter-weary human thousands of years ago standing in this very place and gazing skyward with relief. More than any other sight or sound, the appearance of sandhills means that spring is indeed returning.

## *April*

At sunrise the wetland quickly transforms into bird-call bedlam. Birds call for mates. Birds shout away intruders. Birds in nests scream for food. Now that the flocks of red-winged females have finally appeared, the wetland echoes with the sound of SPIT A CHEW SPIT A CHEW. Meanwhile, red-winged males tirelessly advertise their availability from the highest reed or cattail. Each seems to try to outdo the next, as they sing, spread their tails, and display their red epaulets and plumage to make themselves look bigger.

Meanwhile, the dusky females, who seem streaked and drab compared to the males, have scattered throughout the wetland. Some carry strips of wet cattail leaves to build nests. Others perch on the highest stalks, where they bow and posture. Once couples pair up, the female builds a nest as close to the water as she can. Hidden among the tangle of last year's dry, yellow sedges and toppled cattails, these cuplike nests are sometimes sloppily rigged and woven between stalks. The water's edge is often a precarious place to raise a family that cannot swim, but as long as the nest does not take a nose-dive, it's out of reach of most land-roving predators, such as foxes and coyotes.

The red-winged blackbird is one of several birds that have developed handy wetland courtship and nesting skills. Red-wings can land on two slippery, vertical marsh reed stalks, grip one with each foot, and still manage to sing. The marsh wren, like the red-wing, also uses thick cattail or hard-stemmed bulrush to build nests over water. The more secretive, buff-colored sedge wren makes its nest deep in tall sedges, where it can find plenty of insects to eat. Agile, noisy male wrens often build large numbers of dummy nests in the cattails to attract more than one female. The chunky, dark swamp sparrow also finds cattails handy for conspicuous song perches and nest sites.

Sly, secretive birds prefer the wetland to raise their young because there are so many good places to hide a nest among the thick vegetation. The shy pie-billed grebe is a solitary bird that constructs low, wet nests among rotting cattails, which provide eggs with heat and humidity.

Virginia rails are rarely seen small birds with long reddish bills. They skulk and nest hidden away in the deepest, thickest part of the wetland. They seldom fly and prefer to escape intruders by running and vertically flattening their bodies to pass among vegetation.

Only the BUTTER-BUMP, BUTTER-BUMP call of the least bittern gives away its location. This rarely seen bird builds isolated, delicate nests several feet above the water in cattails and feeds upon frogs. When in danger, the bittern freezes on its nest with its long, thin tawny neck extended to blend in with surround tall sedges.

Birdwatcher and writer Charles Wendell Townsend stumbled upon four young bitterns deep in a marsh in 1913 and mistook their perfectly still, outstretched necks for "stakes of a dilapidated gunner's blind." When he came closer, the young bitterns gave up their deceptive pose, "snapped their bills loudly in anger, erected the feathers of their necks, spread their feeble pin-feathered wings and, emitting faint hissing snarls, sprang defiantly at me."

Every spring, Canada geese, who mate for life, return to the same wetland where they were born. Geese build nests on mats of bulrushes or the tops of muskrat houses where there's a good view of approaching hungry skunks and coyotes. In early April the female lays four to seven dull, creamy white eggs, which hatch in a month. Within twenty-four hours, the goslings leave the nest. They will spend the next year with their parents, grazing on wetland grasses, roots, and seeds and feasting on aquatic insects and larvae.

Large social birds, Canada geese are seldom alone. By flying, eating, and nesting in groups, they help protect one another. To communicate, they produce a large number of sounds—ranging from an adult's hiss ("Alarm's nearby!") or honking in flight ("Follow me!") to a baby goose or gosling's light, soft repeated chirp ("Thank goodness, my mother found me!").

## Entering the Center

Without warning, warm weather arrives. The sky is bright blue and clear. Tender new grass and reeds prick upward. Mosquitoes hover. A sense of urgency fills the air. Every plant hurries to be first to burst and wriggle into welcome sunlight. Every animal and insect seems hungry and eager to find food and a mate.

With my camera slung around my neck, I drag the kayak through black, sticky mud to the stream. Along the path I find a brilliant yellow clump of marsh marigolds—the first spring wetland flowers. A sleepy garter snake lounges on a nearby tussock.

In spring as many as a dozen sleepy garter snakes may crawl out of the den they shared all winter in a hole beneath a rock or log. The ball of snakes, whose tangled components range from eighteen to thirty inches in length, hibernate together all winter. I've found garter snakes curled up in corners of our basement—a perfect place to hibernate, though a shocking discovery for the fainthearted.

The yellow-striped garter snake beside the marigolds may be warming itself in the sun before going in search of a mate or a meal of frog or fish. Garter snakes are intrepid hunters and fearless swimmers. Their fixed, unblinking eyes are protected with a special transparent layer of skin to help them spot moving prey. Their forked tongues flick in and out of their mouths to help them taste-smell the location of prey. If I look carefully I'll see that the snake has no external ear openings; instead it senses what's going on by being supersensitive with its entire body to vibrations transmitted from the ground.

The ground shakes and quivers and gurgles as I walk. Water seeps over the tops of my boots. Around my ankles swim black, tiny creatures no bigger than the point of a pencil. Hundreds of tadpoles!

Thousands of tadpoles! Their tails flail. They crash into one another in their blind rush to get out of my way.

Each spring frog and toad babies undergo and amazing transformation. An individual female lays more than 20,000 clear, colorless eggs in strings or rafts that float in shallow puddles. These mothers don't wait around to take care of their babies. They simply hop away.

A month later, the eggs that have been clinging to underwater grass stems hatch into squirmy tadpoles. At first the helpless tadpole is a little blob with a tail, sightless eyes, no mouth, and feathery gills. It clings to an underwater piece of grass. Eventually its mouth opens and it develops a horny beak and rasping teeth that it will use to find vegetation to eat. Eyes develop. Little by little, two small hind legs appear. Front legs sprout, then lungs form. Eyes grow bigger, stick out from the head, and develop protective eye lids. The tail disappears. By the time summer arrives and all the massive changes in skin, bones, and external organs are complete, the young frog or toad hops on to dry land.

I dump water out of my boots and trudge deeper into the wetland. A northern leopard frog, sensing my footsteps, leaps and zigzags. *Splash!* Where did it go? The frog's camouflage patchwork blends in with the mud and grass at the stream's edge. It holds perfectly still. Only its bulging eyes stick up above the water. *ZIP! ZIP!* The frog scissor-kicks and vanishes.

I push the kayak into the stream. The knee-deep mud is soft and thick as cornmeal batter. I step into the kayak and take a seat. When I lift my paddle, I scoop up shredded bits of reed stems, pieces of crayfish, cattail fluff, old roots, rotted blossoms, leaves.

Something floats past. A turtle? No. It's an entire uprooted cattail plant. Somewhere upriver a muskrat must be busy doing what he does best: eating. I decide this morning to go on a hunt to take a photograph of one of these elusive creatures.

In the next several hours of pausing and waiting and paddling from spot to spot along the lake shore and stream bed, I find nothing. Not one muskrat.

Discouraged and frustrated, I make my way from the lake back to the stream and the boat landing. So much precious time wasted,

I tell myself. *You should be back at your desk—working.* But no—
I'm out here, not finding anything I'm looking for, accomplishing
nothing.

The nose of the kayak bumps into the bulrushes and stops. I'm
about to crawl out, when for some odd reason I glance south. I don't
know why. Maybe it's because of bird song. Maybe it's the movement in the cattails. Whatever the reason, I pause. I've never been
upstream beyond the boat landing before. In winter it's too unsafe to
travel this way because underwater springs ensure that the ice never
freezes completely. In early summer it's too difficult and narrow to
make the journey because water lilies and sedges grow so thick along
the narrow passageway.

What if I head upstream right now? After all, I've already wasted
several hours. What will another hour in the kayak matter? This
might be my only chance.

I begin to paddle upstream.

The stream meanders south into a very wild, pristine fifty-one-
acre fen—an ancient word that first appears in the 1,200-year old
epic poem *Beowulf.* Fen in old English means "marsh, dirt, mud." In

Bright marsh marigolds bloom first in spring.

*Beowulf* the fen is the monster Grendel's loathsome lair, a place so treacherous that no warrior is brave enough to enter. "Seek if you dare," the wise king warns heroic Beowulf as he's about to track down the monster in that perilous place, "the secret land, the wolf-slopes, the windy headlands, the dangerous fen-paths."

*"Seek if you dare."*

A good warning. And yet one I choose to ignore.

I paddle on through the fen, a wetland with a calcium-based soil and limestone-fed springs that support unusual grasses like beaked spike-rush and endangered kittentails. It's impossible to walk very far in a fen because the ground in many places has the consistency of pudding. If you take a wrong step, which is likely, you can find yourself up to your neck in mud without any way to get out.

*"Seek if you dare."*

The twisting, turning stream becomes narrower and narrower. On either side of me bristle thick stands of rattling dry cattails as stout as a child's wrist. The cattails rise up six feet or more. I must use the kayak paddle as a pole to push myself forward against whatever solid clumps I can find.

The water beneath the kayak flows limpid clear and cold and surprisingly deep. Red-winged blackbirds dive-bomb and shout insults at me.

I keep moving upstream.

I can't see where I'm going. I can't turn around. I have no idea what lies ahead.

When the way becomes too narrow, I grab hold of the cattails and haul myself and the kayak forward. Suddenly, overhead roars a 747-sized sandhill crane. Six-foot grey wingspan, yellow eyes, long, trailing prehistoric legs fill the space above me. For a moment, I catch a glimpse of the crane's sharp beak. My ears ring with the bird's warning cry, a harsh clamor that can only mean one thing: "Stay away from my hidden nest!"

Terrified, I struggle to scoot along faster.

*"Seek if you dare."*

I tug the next bunch of cattails with greater care. Now I imagine that each stalk, each bunch of bulrush conceals teeth, beaks, claws—the unsuspecting jaws of a terrified river otter or perhaps the beaked mouth of a furious snapping turtle.

On and on I float through the long, rattling passageway—conscious only of forward movement. I'm unaware of time, oblivious to thirst, unconcerned what I will do if I overturn and become trapped here. No one knows where I am.

I keep pushing myself along. The kayak passes over beds of white shells half-buried in the mud and the first tight pink underwater fists of water lilies about to unfold. The fen smells of the ocean—a fishy, windblown, salty smell.

Just when I'm about to lose hope I'll ever find the end of the passageway, the great blinding barrier of thick cattails suddenly vanishes. The stream opens up into a quiet, secret inlet in the middle of the fen—an unexpected refuge of overarching sky, darting swallows, bright sunlight, and new growth quavering beneath the clear water. Has anyone besides geese or frogs or freshwater mussels ever been here before?

I drift a long time trying to calculate where I am in relation to the outside world and how far I might have traveled. None of this matters. By accident—by mere chance really—I have traversed some boundary, and something sacred seems to have revealed itself. I have entered the center. The landscape I did not know existed—the heart of the fen. And for the first time, I feel as if the wetland knows I'm here.

I'm muddy, weed-spattered, wet. Muskrat-eye deep in the bulrush, I've gone as far as I can into the interior of the fen. I can't paddle any further. I certainly can't get out and walk any further. And yet I'm content. I have become the wetland.

I'd like to stay here a very long time. But the sun is starting to shift, the day is growing late, and my family does not know where I am. When it comes time to actually return, I wonder how I can describe this place. What can I say? How can I communicate this mystery? Who'll understand?

*"Seek if you dare."*

I turn the kayak around and paddle back, downstream this time. I pull the kayak into the landing, clamber out, and drag the boat and paddle up the muddy path back to the barn. Only later the next day, when I walk down the road that runs along the rim of the fen, do I try to peer with binoculars into the distance to see where I was. I can't detect a hint of the opening. Hidden among the reeds and cattails, the secret inlet seems to have vanished as completely as a dream.

### Early Wanderings on the Edge

The first raccoons out of their dens in early spring are hungry males looking for something to eat and a mate. Because raccoons know how to swim (although they'd rather not), they can live and sleep in wetlands—usually in abandoned muskrat houses. Here they have ready access to their favorite foods: crayfish. But raccoons aren't picky. They delight in whatever's available—berries, fresh water snails, frogs, snakes, salamanders, dragonfly larvae, grasshoppers, duck eggs, ducklings, and baby muskrats.

The sense of touch is important to this clever, curious nighttime hunter and forager. Scientists think raccoons dip their food in water before eating in order to improve their ability to feel and identify their meal.

One morning at dawn I discover a raccoon wobbling in a tipsy fashion up from the wetland. The raccoon waddles to the bird feeder beside the barn. It hoists itself up on to a nearby wall, like a thirsty drunk, tips the bird feeder back, and guzzles a stream of sunflower seeds—without one chaser of water.

So much for scientific observation.

## *May*

High over the wetland, big bruise-colored storm clouds gather. Sandhill cranes send up a loud shout. From my lookout on a nearby hill I watch the wind flatten and winnow the bulrush and sedges like a comb through damp hair. *Hsssss!* I shiver from the sudden smack of cold air. A flock of swallows swoops like one bird and dashes for cover among the trees at the wetland's edge.

Thunder grumbles. The sky darkens. Lightning cracks and sizzles. The lake turns flat metallic grey. Only one bird remains on the water. The mute swan's brilliant white color seems to declare: "Just try and strike me!"

Rain stampedes through the bending reeds and sends up the heady smell of dust and tender grass. Rippling puddles overflow. The lake swells. The stream bulges.

And as suddenly as the rain appears, the storm clouds move off beyond the next hill. The sky clears. The grass glistens. A loud, boastful red-wing soars out of hiding and sings *CONK-LA-REE!* as proudly as if it had created the wetland's rainbow all by itself.

### Effigy Mounds, Chimera, and Other Encounters

Finding any kind of record that reveals how indigenous people 1,500 years ago viewed wetlands may seem as impossible as pinning down a chimera. No written record, no surviving oral story, no cave painting survives that might help.

And yet scattered beside wetlands and rivers throughout central and southeastern Wisconsin—in some places less than fifteen miles from where I live—survives a remarkable array of monuments dedicated to powerful water spirits. These impressive earthen sculptures, effigy mounds, vary in size from 5 to 6 feet in height and from 20 to 1,300 feet in length. Their myriad shapes have been described by perplexed early European and American observers as hawks, bears, buffalo, turtles, panthers, and snakes.

Of the 1,863 identifiable zoomorphic mounds recorded in 1998 by the Office of the Archaeologist of the State Historical Society of Wisconsin using nineteenth-century drawings, survey notes, and current remnants, 37 percent are believed to represent water spirits. The survey reports that of the rest, 34 percent are birds, 15 percent are bears and bearlike forms, and the remainder are classified as "various kinds of animals."

Effigy mounds are believed to have been built by indigenous people during what's arbitrarily called the Late Woodland culture that flourished in this part of Wisconsin 2,500 to 850 years ago. At this time many changes were occurring. Indigenous people replaced spears as primary hunting and fighting tools with new technology, such as bows and arrows. Indians at this time created pottery with especially ornate belief-system symbols. They adapted corn as a domesticated plant introduced from civilizations in Mexico. This crop would be later supplemented with beans. Village-based farming was slowly becoming a way of life, although hunting and gathering in smaller, nomadic bands served as a regular seasonal endeavor. In the midst of these shifts in economic and settlement patterns was a flowering of effigy-mound building.

For Late Woodland people and those who came before them, wetlands in southeastern Wisconsin were bountiful places where ducks, fish, and birds could be found. Wetlands provided wild rice harvests. They were rich resources for plants used for food or to make household items, shelters, and medicines. They were a place to meet with other bands to celebrate.

It should not be surprising, then, that ridges and hills above wetlands and their connecting streams, rivers, and lakes were the places Late Woodland people created spectacular effigy mounds. The long-tailed shapes of water spirits, which look eerily like the shadows of mudpuppies, newts, and salamanders, are commonly found slithering away from or toward what were once fertile wetlands and waterways. These were places to celebrate rituals of renewal for people dependent on hunting and gathering.

The effigy mounds, many anthropologists believe, are in fact large cosmological maps that reflect the upper and lower world images that appear in later Native American iconography: thunderbirds represent the upper world; water spirits represent the lower world; and bears represent the land. Mound builders may have created these images to symbolize balance in the forces of life. Each cluster of water spirits, archaeologist Robert Birmingham and forensic anthropologist Leslie E. Eisenberg note in *Indian Mounds of Wisconsin,* contain upper world images. Each cluster of birds also includes a water-spirit or snake image to keep the group in harmony.

Recent studies by archaeologists and anthropologists have revealed fascinating insights about these early cultures and their cosmological views of the universe. Bird effigies with outstretched wings are found most frequently near the rugged hills and bluffs of western Wisconsin. Shapes of bears are most commonly located among mounds in central and western Wisconsin. Water spirits are the dominating image in watery southeastern Wisconsin. And yet, whatever forms predominate in the effigy mound groupings, the opposite world is always represented.

The effigy mounds were perhaps expressions of awe and served as a kind of resource map celebrating the life-giving bounty of the streams, rivers, lakes, and surrounding wetlands. The mounds may also, according to anthropologist R. Clark Mallam, have been "metaphorical expressions of social relationships." He describes them as ideals to be maintained in the larger Late Woodland community. "What the mounds symbolize," Mallam writes, "is balance and harmony—idealized natural and cyclical regularity—and the forces of life which were critical to production."

Among the Late Woodland people, effigy building was an ongoing activity involving tons of soil and much hard work over many years. The construction may have helped build solidarity among kinship groups. The process of attempting to achieve balance and understanding through mound building can be compared to the Navajo practice of continually "thinking and singing the world into existence," described by Gary Witherspoon in *Language and Art in the Navajo Universe*. Each effigy cluster is as unique as the people who constructed it.

Today, most of the effigy mounds have vanished: plowed over for farms, dug up for house foundations, or leveled for road construction. And yet the soil shadow of a huge bird with a 1,300-foot wingspan can still be seen in an airborne photograph taken in 1968 above a Wisconsin field. A few valiant individuals have attempted to save the mounds, realizing their archaeological and spiritual importance. Among the most renowned is Wisconsin pioneer scientist and Renaissance man Increase A. Lapham (1811–1875), who traveled between 1836 and 1852 to map and chart mounds before they were plowed over and destroyed.

What strikes me when looking at Lapham's laboriously correct drawings (he was a surveyor by training) is how often water-spirit images with long tails appear. Lapham calls them turtles or panthers—neither of which title seems to fit. No turtle has a tail that long, and panthers never visited this part of Wisconsin. In a kayak looking down into the water I can see how much Lapham's drawings reflect

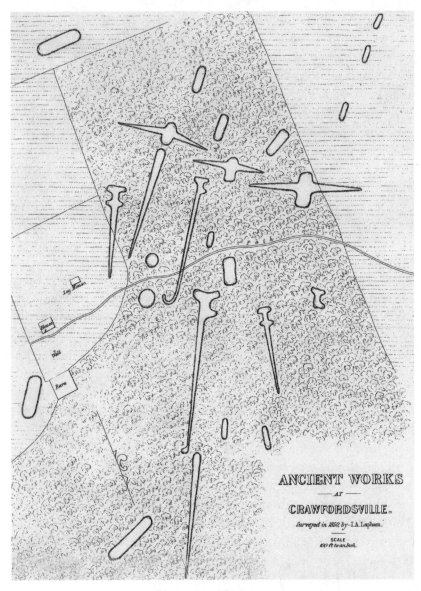

The creature-shaped mounds in Lapham's sketches labeled "Crawfordsville" (later renamed Dewey) appear to be heading away from the wetlands of the Fox River. (I. A. Lapham, *The Antiquities of Wisconsin, as Surveyed and Described,* facsimile of 1855 edition [Madison: University of Wisconsin Press, 2001], plate 16.)

the shapes of frogs and polliwogs, water bugs, and nymphs. There is such a striking resemblance between salamander shapes and the water-spirit design. When I look up into the sky at a sandhill crane or a hawk flying directly overhead, I can make out effigy bird outlines. And soon everything I see casts a shadow that reflects the mounds' mysterious shapes.

Spring as a time of renewal seems the best season to view the effigy mounds—before vegetation becomes too overgrown and the mound shape is obliterated. On an early May morning I decide to try to find what might be left of a group of effigy mounds that at one time included six water-spirit shapes.

The mounds are located twelve miles from here, in Waukesha County. The Dewey Mounds, as they are known, were located on what was once the Bornfleth brothers' farm in Sections 21 and 28 in the town of Vernon in Waukesha County. A family named Dewey formerly had owned the land, hence the mounds' name.

I drive north on County L through hills, past dairy farms, and along an upland to a dead-end road marked Mound Road. At the end of the road are a large farmhouse, a barn, and a pasture for cows. Beyond that lies a field of corn that stretches north, downhill toward the Fox River. It is an impressive vista. I have to imagine fewer trees to block the view of the river. The wind blows. A rooster crows when I get out of the car. I knock at the door of the large house. No one answers—not even a vicious farm dog.

The tenant in the smaller house nearby answers the door and walks me back to the pasture fence. She's a friendly young woman and says some people from University of Wisconsin–Milwaukee were here a few months earlier with a large book, searching for burial mounds. She points in the direction that they were looking. "The mounds are out there someplace in that pasture," she says.

Beyond the wire fence enclosure stand a few scraggly trees—scant shade for a cow pasture. Near one side of the pasture, I spy the place where a humped shape about three feet tall is now covered with small shrubs and grass. It's hard to picture a tail, a head, or a wing because of so much overgrowth. I can't walk farther than the fence because the owner hasn't given me permission to enter the pasture.

I scan the ridge down the place where the Fox River, or the Pishtaka (as Native Americans called it), runs behind the grove of trees. Lapham wrote that the Indians called all rivers with numerous short bends by this name "from the resemblance of their course to that of a fox when pursued." At one time, Late Woodland people may have grown corn interspersed with beans nearby on small, scattered hillocks.

The young woman waits patiently for me to finish taking a photograph. "Have you ever noticed anything out your back window in this direction in winter when snow covered the ground?" I ask.

"No," she says. "Of course I didn't know the mounds were there."

I wish I had a helicopter—or at least a very tall ladder—for a better look. Reluctantly, I leave, thanking her for her help. I go home and study Lapham's drawings.

In Lapham's 1850 sketch, which he labeled "Crawfordsville," a wetland stretches on either side of the Fox River. On the ridge that curves beside the river he included nearly thirty effigy mounds varying in height from two to six feet. They appear to be clambering or flying away from the wetland and the river. Three birds with outstretched wings nearly a hundred feet wide fly south away from the Fox River almost wing-tip to wing-tip. Behind the birds are three water spirits, followed by three long-tailed four-legged creatures; a lone bear shape; and, bringing up the rear, a snake shape. Interspersed among the animals are a dozen oblong hills of various sizes.

Isaac Bailey was already living on the place when Lapham came here in 1850; he included Bailey's house, well, and barn beside a path in his drawing. The spot was supposed to become the site of a town, Crawfordsville, which never was built. Several of the mounds were hidden in Bailey's wood lot.

"I have endeavored to represent these monsters as they appear upon careful survey and plotting," wrote Lapham of the cluster. "They occupy ground sloping gently towards the river at the north and northwest, their heads pointing up hill, and their general course southwesterly. The winged mounds or dragons (three in number) appear to lead the flight or march of the other animals, and to be heralded by a host of simple oblong figures, extending nearly half a mile in the same direction."

Lapham described the main figure in the group as 286 feet in length, a "lizard." The other two figures, according to Lapham, "having four projections or feet, are always called turtles by the most casual observer."

It must have seemed strange to Lapham, who had typical, negative attitudes about wetlands so common in the nineteenth century. He seems to wonder aloud why any group of people would have gone to so much trouble to locate monuments near such a swampy place. "This locality," he wrote, "was doubtless of much importance to the original inhabitants. It is protected on three sides by the marshy grounds along the margin of the river."

Not understanding or making the connection between early indigenous cosmology and symbols, Lapham, like so many other nineteenth-century scientists, dubbed the long-tailed creatures "panthers." He wondered if the other figures with short stubby legs and enormous tails might be turtles. Lapham speculated that the mounds were burial sites "of some distinguished family." When various excavations took place during the next 150 years, however, no corpses were found inside them.

Thanks to Lapham's stubborn fascination and curiosity, we know what we little we do know about the "winged mounds or dragons" of the Dewey Mounds. "It is very much to be hoped," wrote Lapham, "that the good taste of the present intelligent proprietor will induce him to preserve them from destruction."

Lapham's flattering prediction would unfortunately not come true. The land changed hands numerous times. During the 1920s and '30s, the Dewey family owned the property. In April 1923, Charles E. Brown, secretary of the Wisconsin Archaeological Society, published an article about the site. At that point, a number of the mounds had already been destroyed by cultivation. Brown described the water spirit shapes as turtles, a common description at the time.

"Of the panther effigies," wrote Brown, "one was peculiar in having the tip of its long tail curved upward and one had a small knob at the end of its tail. The third was of the very common form, having a long tapering tail ending in a point. Two of the linear mounds were of the long tapering type, the others of the common straight parallel sided form."

In spite of studies by the Wisconsin Archaeological Society and various community leaders who in the 1940s and 1950s tried to spur interest in creating a park to preserve all the mounds, nothing was done. The wood lot was thinned. New houses were built on the perimeter. Some of the mounds were trampled by cows, plowed over for corn fields, or intersected by roads.

Local resident Donald E. Hollister tried for many years to create a park to preserve the mounds as "hallowed ground," as he wrote in November 1956. Sensing the effects of skyrocketing population growth in the Milwaukee metropolitan area, he commented prophetically, "Such a wave has in the past, and can again, destroy the works of nature and of man. The Dewey Mounds should be preserved and protected for what they are—the visible historical evidence of a former civilization about which there is as yet only fragmentary evidence."

In 1990, Randall and Jane Craig bought the farm containing the remains of the mounds. Craig's relatives have lived in this part of Wisconsin since 1840. He was born and raised on the farm west of the Dewey Mounds. When I spoke to him, he said that about twenty mounds are left, surrounded by a pasture fence on the six acres just west of the barn and house. "The mounds look like birds with long tails," he said. "It's kind of hard to see now because of the grass."

Over the years the Craigs have had various visitors investigating the mounds, including a group of students from Carroll College and a retired engineer from University of Wisconsin–Madison. The engineer checked the actual configuration of the mounds against the Lapham drawings using GPS equipment. What fascinated Craig was the long row of black granite rocks that the engineer discovered nearby. "As a kid I always thought those rocks were just part of a stone fence," admits Craig, who found many arrowheads when he was a boy out plowing.

The engineer checked their alignment of the rocks and noticed that they pointed straight north toward the effigy mounds. The last rock at the end, Craig said, was made of limestone. "There's a hole augured in it."

He's never seen any vapors or strange disturbances out in the pasture. At the same time, he has no intention of ever turning the mound land into crops. "They shouldn't be plowed up," he says, then chuckles. "Who knows? May be bad luck."

### Native Americans in the Wetlands: Making Use of Nature's Bounty

Who camped on this hill and used this wetland for hundreds of years prior to the first documented contact with Europeans in the early 1600s?

It's impossible to know with any certainty. The reason is that even *before* the actual arrival of Europeans in what's now Wisconsin, their trade goods, diseases, and technology were already having a profound impact here. A ripple effect of displacement and conflict washed like a wave from the tribes along the East Coast, who first experienced contact, to those living in the Great Lakes region. Much of the earliest recorded observations about tribes in Wisconsin came from French fur traders and missionaries—not always the most reliable sources because of language problems, prejudice against Native American customs and religion, and the fact that by the time French records were made, social disruption was already in full swing here.

Those tribes who can be identified as most likely to have lived in southeastern Wisconsin prior to the early 1600s include Ho-Chunk (Winnebago) and Menominee. According to different accounts, the Potawatomi first occupied southeastern Wisconsin by the end of the 1600s. Undoubtedly, over time many different tribal groups may have used this wetland and the surrounding area to hunt, gather food, and set up homes. No tribe ever claimed to own the land; this was a concept Europeans brought with them.

What is known for certain is that the tribes in this area moved around quite a bit. In summer and winter they stayed in villages where they grew corn, beans, and squash and lived in houses made of bark or woven mats of reeds and cattails. In fall and spring they divided into smaller groups to hunt, fish, or gather sap for sugaring operations in maple groves. Whether these smaller groups were extended family groups, no one is certain. The village social organization revolved around lineage, people descended from one known individual who might be a woman or a man.

Clans traced their ancestry beyond that to a spiritual source, usually an animal or some part of the landscape. This gave certain individuals the rights to perform certain rituals with medicine bundles. Through these clans, strangers were brought into the community. Among the Ho-Chunk and Menominee, individuals were divided into clans identified with earth or sky. These divisions helped organize rituals, leadership, and war parties.

Prior to European contact, Native Americans roasted their food; steamed it in pits; or boiled it in pottery jars or by adding hot stones to clay, bark, or wood containers filled with water. They made their clothing of cured hides or furs.

The wetland was a bountiful place to find many things that the Native Americans needed to live. In addition to game such as bison, deer, moose, bear, beaver, muskrat, and rabbits, the wetland attracted waterfowl and turtles. Fish were plentiful—even during the winter months, when tribes used spears to ice fish.

Wetland plants were used extensively as food, shelter-making supplies, and medicines. What could be found in the wetland, when was the best time to gather the plant, and how to use it was knowledge passed down from generation to generation, from tribe to tribe. Huron L. Smith and S. A. Barrett gathered a remarkable collection of indigenous uses of wetland plants from Menominee and Potawatomi informants in the early part of the twentieth century for the Milwaukee Public Museum.

*Black-eyed susan,* called "memakate 'ningweuk" or "black eyeball" by Potawatomi, blooms in late summer in sedge meadows. Potawatomi boiled the small flowers or florets inside the head of the black-eyed susan with water to create a yellow dye. They dried roots of the plant to make a tea for curing colds.

Potawatomi scraped inner bark from *black spruce,* called "kawa' ndag" or "coarse evergreen," to make into a poultice for inflammation when infection was suspected.

*Blue flag,* also known as blue iris, grows in the wetland in spring. It is called "pakwiasko ns" or "water weed" by Potawatomi. Many tribes discovered that the thick roots could be pounded into soothing poultices for inflamed skin sores. Native women picked blue flags' strong, flat, smooth leaves and wove them with the stems of rushes to make mats and baskets.

*Bulrush,* called "ana'gûnûsk" or "mat weed" by Potawatomi, was used for mats and baskets. Women gathered stems in early summer. They favored smaller stems with narrower pith cavities because these made stronger mats. Women bleached the stems by soaking them in lake water. After the stems were dried, women dyed and wove them together with cord made from basswood to create mats used as floor coverings, house partitions, and special places for food during feasts. Weavers created wigwam mats of different patterns that averaged thirty by sixty inches in size.

*Cattail,* known as "aba' kweûck" or "shelter weed" and "biwiê shwînûk" or "fruit for baby's bed," had a number of uses. Potawatomi harvested cattail stalks in the fall. They trimmed these and laid them out to dry in the sun. They peeled off the outer layers of the stalks and cut them into even lengths, then laid them parallel on the ground and sewed them together using a special bone needle with a basswood cord. By carefully sewing the edges to avoid unraveling, mat makers fashioned waterproof, windproof side coverings for the walls of wigwams and medicine lodges. Women split ripened cattail fruit heads to strip fuzzy seed heads used as quilts for infants. They stuffed cattail fluff inside papooses as the first disposable diapers. Medicine men plucked and crushed fresh cattail roots to make poultices to ease inflammations.

Potawatomi peeled the inner bark of *elderberry,* called "babachisi ganatik" ("popgun wood"), and steeped this in water to create a powerful purgative.

*Milkweed* was called "anêni'wic" or "man weed" by Potawatomi, who used it as a thread material when the pods were green and just about to open. The rind, or bast fiber, of the bark was considered very strong. They removed the bark by throwing it into a pot of boiling water. Later, white settlers believed that milkweed juice could cure warts.

The distinctive red-cupped leaves of the *northern pitcher plant* are easy to spot in melting snow drifts. In May or June its long-stemmed, purplish-brown flower blooms. The pitcher plant is carnivorous, or insect-eating. A sweet substance on the leaves, which have downward pointing hairs, attracts small bugs. Once the insect lands or crawls down inside the cupped leaves, there's no escape. The special chemicals in the cup's liquid begin to break down the insect's body so the plant can absorb it.

The Potawatomi called the pitcher plant "kokokoo makesin," meaning "owl's toe," and dug up the roots to treat smallpox and lung and liver ailments. They dried pitcher plant leaves for use as fever-relieving teas. Chippewa children called the leaves "frog-leggings" and played with them as toys or filled them with ripe berries.

*Red osier,* a member of the dogwood family, was called "mems-kwakwuk," or "red stemmed bush" by Potawatomi. Bark from osier twigs was peeled, roasted over a fire, chopped, and mixed with tobacco to make "kinnikinnik," which was smoked in peace pipes during special ceremonies. The bark of the red osier root was said to be a cure for stomach aches.

*Water plantain* or broad-leafed arrowhead, known in Potawatomi as "wabasi' binik" or "white potato," produced a starchy, cornlike substance on short lateral rootlets. Native Americans pounded these into a pulp to use in poultices for wounds. The mass of fibrous roots are difficult to dig out because the stems break easily. As a result, tribes often raided the water plantain caches of muskrats in winter, if they could be found.

Arrowhead corns or tubers were cooked in a hole dug in the ground heated with red-hot stones. Five or six bushels of the tubers were placed in the pit and covered with wet moss. The cooking required several days with the rocks reheated as needed. When fully cooked, the tubers were cut into slices and hung from basswood strings to be dried for future use. A tasty dish was made with venison, "potatoes," and maple sugar.

*Water lily* roots were pounded and used as a poultice.

*Wild rice,* called "manomîm" or "good berry" grew in slow moving streams and edges of lakes. In fall Native Americans in canoes went out into the wild rice beds with poles about 12 feet long with a fork at one end. While one harvester reached out with the bent stick to bend the heads of rice into the canoe, the other used a paddle to knock wild rice grains into the bottom of the canoe. They could safely gather about forty pounds at one time.

The rice harvesters then returned to shore to place the wild rice into tubs heated over a fire to parch (not scorch) it. Someone stirred the grain constantly with a wooden paddle. Then it was removed to a trampling pit, where an individual in new moccasins walked on the rice all day to remove the hulls. Next, the rice was tossed into the air so the breeze could carry away the chaff. The rice had a long storage life. When cooked, it expanded three to four times in size. It was sweetened with maple syrup

Roots as well as seeds of *yellow lotus,* called "wagipîn" or "crooked potato," were relished. Two terminal shoots of the roots look like bananas. The starchy root was cut and strung on a basswood string for winter use. Seeds from the lotus were gathered and roasted like chestnuts. Nicholas Perrot, an early Wisconsin visitor, described how Indians dug for the lotus root under the ice in winter. He wrote, "To eat it, you must cook it over a brazier and you will find that it tastes like chestnuts."

## May Chorus

Wild chorus of frogs on a mild, moonless night! The high sleigh bell music of early spring peepers has given way to the calls of lovesick leopard frogs that sound like thousands of rubber balloons being rubbed together. Every so often this music is interrupted by the loose banjo twang of green frogs, the steady low snore of pickerel frogs and the deep-pitched *JUG-O-RUM* of bullfrogs.

"When you (hear) those frogs in spring they are singing and they are crying also for those other frogs that die in winter," Mrs. William Tahwah, a Potawatomi woman from Forest County told Charles E. Brown in 1944. "So that is why they [are] singing crying for them. My grand uncle told me this."

I think about this Potawatomi story when I turn on my flashlight and walk a few steps down the wetland path. Suddenly, the frog "singing crying" stops. I pause, waiting. A few hardy voices begin. And soon the croaking chorus fills the night once more.

Bullfrogs, the largest native frog, grow six to eight inches in length. When looking for a mate it calls in resonant bass notes from shallow water. The bullfrog makes a spit-like *phphoot!* when fighting with other males.

Green frogs, which grow to be about four inches long, like to linger on the water's edge near the boat landing. The male makes an explosive, throaty *GOONK! GUNK! GUNK!* when looking for a mate. When frightened, the green frog leaps from the shoreline and is said to squeal *EEEEK!* before hitting the water.

Northern leopard frogs call night and day during the first warm months. They grow up to five inches long. The leopard frog sometimes wanders from the lake to the soggy wetland. The breeding call is a rattling snore that lasts about three seconds and is followed by a chuckle.

Pickerel frogs are spotted, three inches long, and can be identified by two distinct rows of squarish spots running down their backs. Many birds avoid eating the pickerel frog because of its nasty taste. Naturally, I've never tasted a pickerel frog. I take it on the recommendation of frog authorities. The pickerel frog's mating call is a harsh snore slightly shorter than that of the northern leopard frog. What's remarkable is that the pickerel frog has also been known to call underwater.

Northern spring peepers are small, one and one-half inch long frogs with a dark X on their backs. One of the first frogs to call in spring, they are nearly impossible to locate. In spite of their small size, spring peepers make loud, piercing bird-like peeps repeated about once per second or faster. When angry, they create a short, stuttering trill, *Purreeeek!* In summer, peepers announce rain by calling with a series of harsh squeaks.

### Fire Encounter

The idea that you might have to burn something to make it grow seems incongruous. And yet fire has been a major shaping force of the wetland and surrounding landscape for the past six thousand years.

If I dig deep enough into the muck of the wetland to produce a core sample, I'd undoubtedly find pollen preserved in peat records that would reveal how frequent and important fire was here. Layers of charcoal beneath the peat show extensive early fires sparked by lightning strikes or purposefully set by Native American hunters who used fire to flush out game. Native Americans used fire to drive deer and bison toward watering places and wetlands, where the animals became trapped in the mud and were easier to kill. With enough wind behind a fire, flames raced across the landscape with nothing to stop or slow the inferno except lakes and rivers.

The fascinating thing about fire is the way it has affected the evolution of wetland vegetation and how it stimulates growth and flowering brought about by consumption of dead vegetation. In sedge meadows the well-developed root system of sedges, which look like grass, grows six inches or more below the surface. After a fire, these plants begin to rapidly flourish again.

Atop nearby low hills oaks thrived two hundred years ago because their corky, fire-resistant bark withstood periodic fire storms. Oaks dominated the hills, creating what are called oak savannahs—parklike groves surrounded by prairie grasses. Flames wiped out fast-growing maple, willow, ash trees and other shrubs that couldn't tolerate fire. Meanwhile, on the soggy sedge meadow edges fires kept under control the scrubby willows, spruce, birch, and invasive non-native shrubs.

Since settlement and the suppression of fires, sedge meadows are eventually being invaded by shrubs like red osier, silky dogwood, red raspberry, elderberry, and woody vines like woodbine and poison ivy. This type of wetland community, dominated by shrubs, is called a shrub-carr, an English term. In 50 years or so a shrub-carr, if left unaffected by fire, will be invaded by shade-producing cottonwood, elm, and ash that totally eliminate sedge meadow species.

Studies of sedge meadow wetlands show that fire has its most pronounced effect on new growth the first and second seasons following the burn. Bugleweed and clearweed, both native species, grow in abundance after a burn. Perennial forb cover also increases. Biologists believe the profusion of new growth is caused because fire consumes leaf litter, blackens the land surface, and allows sunlight to directly reach and warm the soil.

At night, without the insulation of leaf litter, soil temperatures tend to be cooler. Fire clears the way for certain species of native plants to become established by "leveling the playing field." Old growth is eliminated. New growth gains a foothold. Amazingly enough in spring, only a few days after a fire, young green shoots are already shooting through the soil.

"Prescribed burns," as they're called, are part of the Nature Conservancy's attempt to help maintain wetlands and protect the species that live there. "Natural flooding was once a common event in many of the wetland areas that surround streams, rivers, lakes and ponds," explains Nancy Braker, Agency Relations Director, Fire and Invasive Species with the Nature Conservancy. Flooding helped reduce the number of trees and shrubs that invade wetlands. "Flood control devices—such as ditches and levees—have been established to use land for agricultural, residential, or industrial purposes. In the absence of regular flooding, many wetlands become overgrown with trees and shrubs." Cutting down trees is one method to maintain the wetland. The other is fire.

It's hard to imagine that plants have historically been dependent upon fire for long-term health and maintenance. Fire suppresses competing trees and shrubs and stimulates growth and flowering brought about by the consumption of dead vegetation.

According to Mike Kost, who has studied sedge meadows after controlled fires managed by the Nature Conservancy, "Important nutrients become more readily accessible to plants when leaf litter is burned, and these contribute to greater plant growth and flowering. Many animal species are attracted to this healthier growth and prefer to graze in recently burned areas."

Because of fire departments, roads, houses, farms and other civilizing influences, fires do not race across the landscape in my neighborhood they way they once did. To experience a burn means observing a controlled prescribed fire organized and staffed by professionals from the Nature Conservancy.

The Nature Conservancy allows only a narrow window of opportunity for this kind of active management of nature preserves. The burns are done in the spring, before nesting of ground birds. Burns are not done year after year, but are carefully spaced to give time for studies of the effects and to allow regrowth to mature.

Burning only a small section at a time every two or three years allows the insects, birds, and animals to escape to another area to live another day, so to speak. Early fires were not so thoughtful. They just roared through the landscape helterskelter. The fire's effect depended on which section was hit, how hard the wind was blowing, how close water was located, and the wetness of sedges and cattails.

One day in early spring I get the opportunity to observe a controlled burn in my own backyard. After several years of discussion with our neighbors, the Nature Conservancy is finally able to convince and coordinate the eight landowners with property encompassing or abutting the 190-acre fen to allow a prescribed burn. Nothing like this number of property owners has ever been involved in a project of this size before and yet there's an inspiring barn-raising spirit about the enterprise. It's as if we all recognize we need to put aside our differences and work together to help save a special place.

Nonnative shrubs like buckthorn and honeysuckle that rim the edge of the fen are slowly advancing on the interior, the Nature Conservancy staff explains to us. "They'll eventually take over completely, crowding out the pitcher plants, marsh blue violet, and Joe-Pye weed," says Conservancy Land Steward Hannah Spaul. "We need to burn the entire fen to keep the invasive shrubs in check."

In March Conservancy crew members scout the site, make maps, and clear vegetation to create firebreaks around a duck blind and an ice shanty. We paddle canoes to safety across the lake. Conservancy crew members extend a firebreak the width of an all-terrain vehicle between the perimeter of several stands of back yard pines and the wetland. Volunteers distribute flyers to other neighbors to explain what will happen. As the day of the burn approaches, my husband, the son of a Chicago fireman, can not help himself. He stretches a long hose from our house down the hill.

For several weekends in a row, the weather does not cooperate. Too much rain. Too much snow. Moisture content in the plants has to be right. Days pass. Too much wind. Finally, one sunny morning in early April a steady wind begins to blow from the northeast. At 10 A.M. four Conservancy staff and thirteen trained volunteers gather at the fen.

Dressed in yellow-orange, flame-proof coveralls and heavy boots, the crew of men and women, mostly in their twenties and early thirties, sport hard hats, special belts with walkie talkies, and emergency tents the same kind forest fighters crawl inside in the West if fires overwhelm them. Each has had extensive training.

Moving in a coordinated line with the wind at their backs, one part of the team sprays the ground with a thin line of flammable material while another group uses crude brooms to coax the fire along into the leaf debris and small shrubs at the wetland's edge. Each member of the group has a special job. Their manager has overseen controlled burns for more than twenty years.

The crew is made up of dedicated volunteers, some of whom have driven from as far away as Illinois. There's nothing out of control about the scene. Escape routes are marked on maps and memorized. All-terrain vehicles equipped with water tanks stand in readiness. And yet there's always the possibility something can go wrong, especially when the burn reaches the wetland where no one's certain about the steadiness of the ground.

The worst mishap in recent memory, one Conservancy staff member tells me, is when one of the crew sank into a bog up to her waist during a routine burn. Luckily, she had a walkie talkie handy and was able to call for help before the flames came too close. The unpredictability of the wind is always a factor on everyone's mind.

I can not help but feel a kind of nervousness. What if something goes wrong? What if our house catches fire? What if my father's pin oak accidentally becomes enveloped in flames?

The wind holds a steady course for the first hour or so. The crew lights another line of fire on the far northeastern edge of the wetland. My daughter and I stand with other spectators on our hill. We watch the distant dance of flames nibble dead vegetation, sticks, and shrubs. Somehow the scene reminds me of the early days of the Civil War, when crowds from Washington, D.C., climbed the hills outside the city with picnic hampers to watch battles.

"All we need are parasols and watercress sandwiches," I tell my daughter.

Hawks circle overhead. They, too, sense the drama—and possible dinner—about to begin. As smoke curls, rabbits and mice dash through the underbrush for safety.

Then the wind begins to pick up speed. The approaching fire ignites an enormous stand of dried cattails, then another and another. Each time howling flames shoot up fifteen feet into the air. Scraggly buckthorn crackles with a noisy *whoosh*. Closer and closer the fire skulks. Flames creep, burst, die, creep, burst, die. Over and over again. Smoke floats skyward. Whenever the fire meets the edge of the stream or the lake there's an elemental moment. Flames' reflections dance on water. Some primeval greeting of forces—constructive and destructive at the same time.

The sun begins to set. The flames arc and ebb, skyrocket and crash in ever wilder, brighter colors. Just when I wonder if the fire will jump the break, it subsides.

The show is over.

A full moon appears. The wetland smolders. My hair and clothing smell smoky.

I wander along the road and inspect the edge of the burn. In the vanishing light the stand of oaks on a hill appear unscathed. Beneath the stand of trees is a root system that creates "grubs" that lay dormant, waiting for the opportunity to shoot skyward when circumstances are right. Young oaks have been known to resprout even after decades of annual burning. After a burn, oak seedlings have less competition from other plants for precious sunlight, more nutrients have been added to the soil, and sunlight reaches and warms up the soil in spring faster, which jumpstarts the growing season.

Early the next morning my husband, daughter, and I go out into the darkened charred stubs to inspect the wetland. It appears as flattened and bristly as a strange, blackened moonscape. And yet in just one week, when I return again, I discover tender green shoots already peeking through the ground. In two more weeks, tussocks sprout new growth and the first green of thousands of cattails no bigger than the tip of my little finger poke skyward.

The Nature Conservancy sends out a team to survey the burn's impressive results. According to their findings, the invasive shrub layer appears to have been knocked back by about twenty-five percent. "We expect to see increased flowering and seed production of many native plant species this year," says Spaul.

She's right. In a little more than a month the wetland is so lush, it's hard to believe a burn ever occurred.

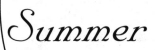

# Summer

Catching the fish was only incidental
to walking along the bank of the creek
and waiting for the sun to set on the marsh.

Richard Quinney,

"A Place Called Home"

# *June*

Brown snout parts the still waters of the lake just around sunset. Behind the snout a humped sleek back cleaves the water with a telltale V-formation. Big as a dog, the beaver ducks under the bed of beheaded spatterdock, ragged pond-lily leaf, then resurfaces with mouth open, moving, chomping. I sit motionless in the kayak watching as one yellow spatterdock blossom after another vanishes like a jawbreaker inside this nocturnal eating machine. Does the beaver realize how ridiculous it looks with a dinner plate–sized lily leaf as a hat?

Luckily, I am downwind of the beaver, which is known for its superb senses of smell and hearing. I hold perfectly still and hope it won't notice me in the drifting kayak. This is the closest I have ever been to a beaver.

Suddenly, a second slick brown head surfaces—this one smaller, swifter—the size of a tomcat. The younger beaver joins its gluttonous companion and eats with abandon. In one day beavers may devour anywhere from one to two pounds of leaves, roots, and bark. While beavers prefer tender tree bark, especially that of aspen, they enjoy nothing so much as fresh water lily blossom, leaf, or starchy root.

The big beaver swims to shore, holding a bunch of lily leaves, roots, and stems clutched in its long-nailed front paws, which appear as nimble and delicate as a precocious child's. The beaver, which probably weighs as much as fifty pounds, waddles to shore, shakes itself vigorously, like a dog, then begins to munch yet another stem. Its bright orange incisors on the top and bottom give it an odd, grinning look of a demented schoolmaster, lacking only wire-rimmed spectacles

Across the lake, tucked against the embankment inside the inlet on the east side, is an enormous beaver lodge that may be this pair's home. The lodge, which has been at the same spot for more than a decade has grown to a height of ten feet and a width of nearly twenty-five feet. This impressive structure of mud and chewed sticks, logs, and branches features at least two underwater entrances for the current colony, which may consist of one breeding pair of adults, several yearlings (one- to two-year-old beavers), and the most recent litter of kits that may have been born between February and June.

With powerful, webbed back feet, a broad, rudderlike tail with leathery scales, nose and ears with valves that close underwater, and eyes with transparent lids that act like swimming goggles, the beaver is nothing short of water-gifted. The beaver can swim at a maximum speed of six miles per hour and stay submerged under water for fifteen minutes. As soon as it dives, its heart rate decreases by half. The beaver's body can tolerate carbon dioxide buildup that would be lethal to humans; this means that the beaver can escape from its enemies by swimming nearly across a lake before coming up for air.

The more I learn about this humble-looking member of the rodent family, the more impressed I am. No other mammal besides the human has changed its environment so dramatically—rerouting streams, flooding grasslands and forests, creating ponds and wetlands. Its not surprising that in so many origin myths, beavers are viewed as critical. The Potawatomi tell how in the beginning when there was nothing but water everywhere, the first man floated in a canoe all alone and dejected. Beaver was one of the first animals to help create land by diving down under the water to bring back piles of mud to make the world.

Beyond the marsh I can find plenty of evidence of beaver handiwork: gnawed stumps of aspen, poplar, and ash trees. The beaver uses its broad tail like a kickstand to keep its body steady as it plunges its sharp, two-inch-long upper teeth into the trunk of a tree. The beaver uses its powerful jaws to gnaw away with its lower teeth; in a matter of minutes, an adult can topple a five-inch-diameter tree. It strips trees clean of bark for food and drags entire trees and large branches to piles along the water's edge. Using its adept front paws, the beaver gathers mud to plaster the logs.

Even after a project is finished, work is ongoing. Beavers patrol dams regularly to make inspections, repairs, additions, and improvements. They constantly monitor and adjust water levels. The depth around a lodge needs to be at least four feet to avoid exposing the colony to danger from predators under the ice in winter. Beneath the muddy lake and stream bottom are weblike underwater passageways and plunge holes dug and regularly dredged by industrious beavers. These are connected escape routes and trails to desirable trees; for although the beaver is swimmer par excellence, its mobility on land is somewhat awkward and slow, making it an easy target for predators or automobiles.

While pairs of beavers mate for life, the colonies themselves are transitory. Groups of beavers shift, change, move away. One study has shown that beaver groups move to new locations every few years. New dams and lodges are constantly being built up and down the watershed. No one knows for certain why the sound of moving water prompts beavers to build dams, but this does seem to be the stimulant that triggers the building instinct.

I watch quietly as the beavers groom themselves. They have special split nails on the inner two claws of each hind foot that they use as a kind of comb. Beavers are meticulous. They spend many hours a day maintaining the waterproof sheen of their thick fur by combing through secretions from scent glands located near their tail. This is the same scent beavers use to mark their territory on mounds of mud. One researcher described the smell as a "sweet musky aroma." Castoreum, as the substance is called, is used as a base for expensive

Wetland beavers have constructed a lodge with poplars, willow, birch, and mud with underwater entrances along the water's edge.

perfume because it combines easily with other fragrances and allows desired scents to release slowly when applied to warm skin.

Beavers were a bountiful resource for early Indians who visited wetlands to hunt. The animals could be easily located—entire families stayed in the same lodge—and were killed with spears or nets or clubs. Beavers were roasted or boiled for food, although early trappers described the flesh as oily and disagreeable. The fat tail, however, likened to cooked chicken, was considered a delicacy.

The beavers' brown fur gleams in the waning sunlight. I am amazed that they have not spotted me, leapt into the lake, and given a thunderous tail-slap alarm against the water as a warning. As I watch them groom their fur with little obvious concern about their own safety, I can't help but think how the beavers' luxurious pelts helped set in motion a remarkable and disastrous course of events for humans and, ultimately, for wetlands throughout North America. Blame it on fashion. Blame it on greed. Blame it on imperialist economics. Whatever the reason, the desire for beaver fur fueled what would become continuous, indiscriminant trapping between 1634 and 1793 that almost led to extermination of the species. In the process, an entire group of indigenous people became dependent on European technology and trade goods—a situation that would spell disaster for their native way of life.

In 1634, ambitious Jean Nicolet, a thirty-six-year-old employee of French explorer, map maker, and fur trader Samuel de Champlain, was sent into the interior of North America. His mission was to make contact with the Ho-Chunk (Winnebagoes), who lived in what's now the Fox River Valley and on the shores of Green Bay. Known to their neighbors as "people of the dirty water," the Ho-Chunk, so Champlain believed, must have once resided near salt water and would be able to give directions to the Northwest Passage that led to the Pacific Ocean and, ultimately, to the rich trade goods of China.

Nicolet left Quebec, followed the shores of Lake Huron, and finally arrived at Lake Michigan. The Frenchman had a flare for drama. He wanted a special ceremony to mark his grand entrance in Green Bay, so he sent word to the Ho-Chunk to get ready. One of the things he had packed (just in case he made it all the way to China) was a flashy damask silk robe embroidered with colorful birds and flowers. He slipped into the robe, careful to attach two pistols to his belt, and stepped ashore before an audience of several hundred Indian villagers. As a flourish, Nicolet shot the pistols into the air and sent everyone scattering.

To show he was friendly, he heaped gifts of mirrors, beads, and cheap hatchets on the ground for the Ho-Chunk. His generosity must have made a big impression. The Ho-Chunk pledged their loyalty to the French in the new enterprise of hunting and trapping for furs, which would involve Hurons as middlemen and extra trade assistance from Menominee, skilled hunters who lived nearby on the Fox River.

Today it is uncertain which tribes lived in Wisconsin around the time of Nicolet's arrival. Three known tribes included: the Siouan-speaking Ho-Chunk (who lived to the west and northwest of Turtle Creek), the Algonquian-speaking Menominee (who lived to the north and east), and the Santee Sioux in the far west, near the Mississippi River.

During warfare that started in the east and spread west during the next two hundred years, the Dutch and French and English supplied guns. Numerous fleeing or displaced tribes eventually leapfrogged into Wisconsin. These included Mascouten, Potawatomi, Sauk, Fox, Chippewa—all of which are woodland-based cultures that had developed agriculture as well. Upheaval accelerated during the 1700s and early 1800s under French, then British, then finally American rule. Tribal populations fluctuated dramatically. Decimated by war, starvation, and disease, tribes fled or moved before they were attacked from woods to prairies and savannas. Tribes were forced to adapt to new hunting techniques, new methods of agriculture.

Nicolet's arrival at Green Bay in 1634 with garish silk robe and startling gunshots was the beginning of the end for the beaver in Wisconsin. From 1660 to 1730, this region became known by the French as one of the best beaver hunting areas in the Great Lakes region. Green Bay was dubbed by one historian as the "beaver emporium" of the state.

When Nicolet and the other first Europeans stepped ashore at Green Bay, they discovered indigenous people using bone awls, flint knives, stone or skin kettles, and bows and arrows. European tools made of iron were extremely attractive to Native Americans. Iron kettles, knives, awls, hoes, axes, guns, powder and shot, and traps were in immediate demand. In exchange, the French and, later, the English and Dutch wanted beaver pelts. Since the mid-1600s beaver hats, made of felt created with the inner hairs of beaver furs, were all the rage for men and women in Europe. "Nothing but beaver stuff or beaver wool shall be used in making of hats," decreed Charles I of England in 1638.

The Europeans' insatiable desire for beaver at first seemed bizarre to Native Americans, who were more likely to eat beaver for meat than use its pelt. "The beaver does everything perfectly well," an Indian trapper told a Jesuit priest in 1657. "It makes kettles, hatchets, swords, knives, bread. In short, it makes everything. The English have no sense—they give us two knives for one beaver skin."

Ten good beaver skins in trade would furnish an Indian hunter with a gun. But of course there was a catch. Tribes that became dependent on European trade goods always needed more: iron tools broke, guns needed repairs, and powder and shot ran out. More disastrous, however, was the invisible "trade" that was made by Europeans, who, often unknowingly, infected entire villages with diseases such as small pox, measles, influenza, tuberculosis, and diphtheria. Native Americans had no immunity to these European epidemics. Mortality in some Indian villages was said to range as high as 90 percent during outbreaks. Meanwhile, intertribal warfare and abuse of alcohol, another European trade good, also took a severe toll.

Technology quickly changed trapping techniques. Using improved metal traps, Indians now killed every single beaver they could find in a colony—a far cry from the pre-European days when they'd be lucky to spear or club one or two. In the course of little more than a century, the population of beavers—which had seemed unending—was nearly wiped out.

By 1763 St. Louis had become the fur-trading capital of the world. In a single expedition, traders would work their way up the Mississippi River with trade goods, meet with Indian trappers, and return with rafts piled high with as many as 30,000 beaver pelts packed in tight 100-pound bundles. The furs were shipped to Europe to be made into expensive hats while the skins were rendered into glue. "The tribes got their trade goods, the traders got rich, and the Europeans got their hats," writes Alice Outwater in *Water: A Natural History.*

By 1793—just thirty years later—there were few beavers left east of the Mississippi or in streams flowing into it. The Menominee, who were considered among the best beaver trappers and hunters, had exhausted all game from their home land around Green Bay and were forced to travel hundreds of miles—into what's now Iowa, the Dakotas, and beyond—to hunt.

By the close of the eighteenth century, beavers in Wisconsin had been nearly wiped out. Only in the far west, beyond the Missouri River and the Rockies, were beavers said to still exist in promising numbers. Thanks to exploration by Lewis and Clark and others, waterways were soon identified and the last vestiges of beaver were trapped.

By 1830, fashions changed. Silk hats were now in demand. The beaver market crashed. But the damage had already been done to the Indians and to the environment. Dwindling in number and in poor health—many suffering from starvation—Indians who clung to this area of Wisconsin faced bleak prospects of little or no remaining game.

To make matters even worse for Indians, their land was quickly being overrun now by a different kind of invader—land-hungry settlers. In March 1835, Solomon Juneau wrote that the Milwaukee Indians were so discouraged by the arrival of "so many settlers north of Chicago that they refused to hunt." Fur companies, now destitute, collapsed in bankruptcy.

The elimination of the beaver and the tragic weakening of the tribal population made what happened next easier for the U.S. government. In 1833 treaties were signed that ceded Indian rights to five million acres of land and set in motion removal, or deportation, of remaining southeast Wisconsin tribes to lands west of the Mississippi River.

In 1839 in Jefferson County, a group of thirty wandering Ho-Chunk families reportedly camped near the home of E. D. Coe on the west bank of the Rock River. Their intention, Coe said, was to try to trap beaver. He doesn't say that they caught anything. In

A beaver enjoys a succulent meal of lily leaf—a favorite food. Photo by Jack Lawlor.

nearby Walworth County, settlers marveled at the size of abandoned beaver dams that now sprouted trees—not colonies of beaver. In 1852 Increase A. Lapham reported that the last beaver in southern Wisconsin had been killed on Sugar Creek in 1819. By the 1880s, beavers in Wisconsin were close to complete extinction. When anyone actually trapped a live beaver, it was considered a news-breaking story by the local press.

As I observe this pair of beavers, I am struck not only by their impact on their environment but their amazing resilience. Before the arrival of Europeans on the North American continent, an estimated 60 to 400 million beavers roamed the North American continent. That number was reduced to near extinction in just two centuries. Little by little, with beaver stock replenishing and hunting restrictions, the beaver has made a steady comeback. Today an estimated 15 million beavers exist in comparatively sparsely settled areas in North America, where they are protected by hunting laws that restrict trapping to certain seasons and areas. I wonder which hardy survivors were this pair's ancestors.

Nothing happens slowly in summer. Now the marsh seems to be on fire, changing every moment. A rush to nest, to flower, to seed. Each time I go away and come back, something's different, something's changed. I can't find marsh marigolds beside the trail anymore. They've been replaced by tall purple spikes of blazing star. Cattails shimmer green and shoot skyward. Nothing stands still. Life in the marsh is a free-fall—a series of ever-moving shadow pictures. Now light, now mottled, now dark. Over and over. Always new, always unexpected, the marsh is like the place Wendell Berry once called, "beautiful, dangerous, abundant, oblivious of us, mysterious, never to be conquered or controlled or second-guessed, or known more than a little."

Among the tribes in Wisconsin who lived near the wetlands and made use of their resources were the Potawatomi, who are an Algonquian-speaking people. They originally came from Canada, according to their legends. Three groups, an alliance called Aui-shinabe or "Original People," crossed into what is now the Upper Peninsula of Michigan. The Great Spirit had assigned each group a task. The Ojibwe (Chippewa) went west as "Keepers of the Faith." The "O-daw-wahg'" (Ottawa) went south as "Trader People." The Potawatomi, "Keepers of the Sacred Fire," went south as well.

By the time Europeans arrived, the Potawatomi had been in southeastern Wisconsin for a century or more. More than two hundred Potawatomi sites have been identified here—everything from villages and sugar camps, cornfields and burial sites, to trails and horseracing tracks. Potawatomi most often selected locations for villages and camps on well-drained hills near lakes, marshes, and streams, where water and resources were readily available.

Simon Kaquados, a well-known Potawatomi leader, described his tribe's earliest agriculture in a 1920 interview: "We cultivated our garden with stone hoes and wooden shovels. In our garden we raised squashes, pumpkins, beans, potatoes, wild corn and onions." Fish, wild rice, muskrats, rabbits, "prairie fowls, roots, Indian corn, and wild fruits" found in or near wetlands were a big part of local Potawatomi subsistence, according to Frank Abial Flower in 1881.

Springs considered sacred by Potawatomi because of medicinal and mineral properties included those at White Rock, Hauk Mineral Rock, and Bethesda Springs (located at what's now Waukesha). Trails connecting wetlands, villages, and hunting areas were visible when Europeans arrived. Later, some of these were transformed into roads—especially where the paths met rivers that had to be forded. Trail-marker trees, many of which featured artificially deformed branches, served to show the direction to be followed. For years bent saplings, which Potawatomi children used as steps to climb on to the backs of ponies, were visible as trail markers.

Potawatomi built their lodges using arched poles, and made the sides from woven bulrush mats and the roofs from tree bark. The Reverend S. A. Dwinnell, who observed Potawatomi in September 1836 near Big Foot village, seventeen miles from here, commented on the permanent wigwams ten feet in diameter made from slabs of bark. Each side had a sleeping platform four feet wide. "Other and more temporary wigwams," he wrote, "were circular and oval. The framework [was] made of saplings and covered with mats woven from rushes and flags [iris]" from wetlands.

Wetlands played a role as refuge, and resource in 1832 during the Black Hawk War, the last armed Indian resistance that precipitated the end of a way of life for Potawatomi and other tribes in this part of Wisconsin.

Years of broken promises and terrible hunger prompted Sauk Chief Black Hawk and his tribe, who had been removed by the federal government to the Iowa shore of the Mississippi, to make a desperate attempt to cross the river and replant their old cornfields. In the spring of 1832, 1,000 warriors, elderly men, women, and children tried to return to their homeland, now occupied by settlers. En route they were stopped by a military force that gave chase. When a small group of warriors sent a delegation with a truce flag to surrender, they were fired upon by Illinois militia.

That hot, wet summer a chase began as Black Hawk took his followers on a long march up the Rock River, skirting the area of lakes near what's now Madison, then down rocky ridges. Black Hawk and his followers hid in wetlands along the way, taking cover and lying low in bulrush. They found waterfowl, fish, berries, and roots that kept them from starving. Brigadier General Henry Atkinson wrote in July 13, 1832, "I am in much doubt whether it will be possible to come up with the enemy whilst he is enabled to subsist on roots & fish taken from the Swamps & lakes."

Black Hawk and his followers moved swiftly through the wetlands, dodging out of sight when soldiers approached. The tribe's ghostlike movements frustrated their heavily laden pursuers traveling with horses, pack trains, and heavy artillery. Rain and mosquitoes plagued the disorganized volunteer militia. Among the soon-to-be famous in this military engagement were future presidents twenty-three-year-old Private Abraham Lincoln and forty-eight-year-old Colonel Zachary Taylor. The chase ended in August 1832 at Bad Axe River, where many of Black Hawk's followers were killed. Black Hawk was later captured and taken to prison in St. Louis. With increasing protest from the public and pressure from white squatters who had already begun to invade Wisconsin land, the U.S. government used the incident to take land from Ho-Chunk, Potawatomi, and Menominee the following year, even though they had nothing to do with Black Hawk's resistance.

The stage was set for the final act in the Indian removal. In 1833, a few years before the Wisconsin Territory was established, the Treaty of Chicago was signed. The Potawatomi gave up five million acres of southeastern Wisconsin and northeastern Illinois in exchange for "certain payments" and five million acres on the east side of the Missouri River in Iowa and northwestern Missouri and Kansas. The Potawatomi were allowed to stay in southeastern Wisconsin three years "without molestation or interruption" after the treaty was signed. Settlers, however, were already trickling into the area to squat on land even before surveys were begun.

In May and June 1838, the remaining area Potawatomi were gathered in Milwaukee to be led west by a pair of trader brothers, Jacques and Louis Viam. Even after their journey, however, the Indians continued to return, hiding in wetlands in an attempt to continue their way of life in Wisconsin. These small, wandering bands slipped in and out of unwanted wetland regions up through the Civil War years.

A painted turtle pauses before diving for cover beneath vegetation. A half dozen or more may bask together sandwich-style atop muddy tussocks.

After that, game declined so dramatically, the Indians' numbers declined as well.

The retelling of this story is based on Potawatomi interviews gathered in the early part of the twentieth century by Alanson Skinner.

### Turtle Goes to War

Snapping Turtle was a well-known brave who had something of a bad temper. One time, when he was acting even crankier than usual, the other turtles said, "Something must be in the air. Snapping Turtle is behaving worse than ever."

A messenger came to the turtles and ordered them to meet at Snapping Turtle's wigwam. "Maybe now he'll be in a good mood," said the turtles. "Who can be cranky while enjoying a feast?"

The turtles went to Snapping Turtle's wigwam and ate and ate. They all had a very good time. When they were almost done feasting, Snapping Turtle made a speech. "My brothers," he said, "I am angry at mankind. I have decided to raise a war-party and fight them."

"Well, certainly there had been insults over the years," the turtles grumbled. "Humans are always making fun of us."

"It's time to do something," Snapping Turtle bellowed. "It's time to fight back."

The turtles felt inspired by such talk from a well-known brave. That very night, while the humans were asleep, the turtles prepared themselves for serious battle. In the morning, they traveled from dawn till dark, and then they rested and slept. During the night Box Turtle had a bad dream. "It's an omen," he told Snapping Turtle. "I don't think we should go into battle,"

"What a fool you are!" Snapping Turtle said angrily. "I don't pay any attention to such omens."

The next day the turtle warriors arose early and traveled from dawn until dark, and then they rested and slept. The next morning each of the turtles sang their dreams and they were all terrible.

Worst of all was Box Turtle's. "Oh, Snapping Turtle, I see you now!" Box Turtle sang. "They are throwing all us turtles in a sack."

"Be quiet!" Snapping Turtle shouted. "We must be on our way." That day they traveled from dawn till dark, and then they rested.

That night Box Turtle kept everyone awake by singing about another terrible dream. So Snapping Turtle, the well-known brave, went up to him and kicked him. Even this did no good. Box Turtle kept singing even in his sleep. Snapping Turtle kicked him again on the breast so hard that he broke Box Turtle's shell, and you may see this break, which became a hinge, to this very day.

"If you value your life," Snapping Turtle warned Box Turtle, "you will sing 'Snapping Turtle, the Brave, he is the one who conquers all villages wherever he goes.'"

"I can't help what I dream," Box Turtle replied indignantly. "I don't want your people put into a sack. This is not my fault. I was asleep, and my dream came out in my song. Who am I to control my dreams?"

Snapping Turtle did not answer. He ordered the turtles to keep moving. At last they arrived at the humans' village. The turtles gave a mighty war whoop and charged. The only turtle lagging behind was Box Turtle, who had been badly injured by Snapping Turtle's kick.

"Look!" cried the women, who ran out of their wigwams. "What luck! The turtles are coming our way!" Excitedly, they grabbed sacks to use to collect the turtles. PLUNK. PLUNK. PLUNK. They dropped in the turtles one by one. The only one that escaped capture was Box Turtle, because he was too slow.

"See this pretty turtle!" said one woman. She picked up Painted Turtle, who was decorated with bright red. As soon as the woman hugged him close, he bit off her nipple.

"Ow!" the woman cried angrily and threw Painted Turtle into the lake, where he quickly swam away underwater. So this one, indeed, counted a coup on the enemy.

The women carried the turtle captives home and were very angry about Painted Turtle's coup. The women held a council over Snapping Turtle, who bragged that he was a well-known warrior. One woman said, "Let's burn this turtle leader, for he is our enemy."

"Hau!" said Snapping Turtle. "That would be good!"

"No," said the women, "this war leader is too desirous to die in this way. Obviously, he thinks in his heart he will be able to kick the fire all over and thus destroy our lodges."

"Let us shoot him with arrows," another woman suggested.

"Hau!" said Snapping Turtle. "Indeed you have discovered the best way!"

"No," decided the women. "The arrows will glance off. What if we're wounded accidentally as a result?"

"Let us then boil him in the great earthen kettle," another woman said.

*"Inneh,"* said Snapping Turtle, "In that way I would die gladly."

"No," announced the council of women, "He thinks that he will be able to spatter boiling water over us and scald us to death."

"In that case," said another, "let us throw him in the lake."

At these words, Snapping Turtle and all his followers began to beg for mercy. "Do not drown us!" they cried. "This is an awful punishment!"

The council of women decided that they had come up with a

perfect plan. So they tossed every turtle into the lake. PLUNK. PLUNK. PLUNK.

The turtles swam away and had a victory dance at Snapping Turtle's wigwam. Painted Turtle was the hero, because he alone had counted coup and touched the enemy and escaped unharmed.

(Adapted from *Turtle Goes to War* [Native title: "Mishi'kä Andopänit"], Potawatomi oral telling collected by Alanson Skinner [*Bulletin of the Public Museum of the City of Milwaukee* 6 (1927), 356].)

## Summer Solstice

Late night thunderstorm drenches everything. In the morning a shy Blanding's turtle miraculously appears up the hill from the marsh. This elusive turtle is a threatened species in Wisconsin that feasts on earthworms, slugs, berries, and grasses while on land. Named for William Blanding, an Illinois turtle collector, it's a marvelous wanderer. It has headed out of the lake, through the wetland, and up the hill to look for a place to nest. According to turtle experts, Blanding's turtles most often search for nests during rainy weather.

This turtle seems to remember this spot from some other life, some long-ago infancy. Blanding's turtles are creatures of habit. They go back to the same place every year to lay their eggs. I wonder how many times she has climbed the hill to find this place. The scrubby area rimming the wetland and the woods beyond are no impediment to this traveling creature, who scurries through leaf litter and around branches with determination.

On her journey, which may have been as long as a mile and a half, she has accumulated a frumpy collection of cattail fuzz around her neck. Her shell crawls with ants, which don't seem to bother her. She has a distinctive yellow chin and a long neck, with a smooth, blue-black carapace flecked with small, yellow marks that almost look like paint splatters. (Only when she was five years old did her chin turn yellow.) Her head, tail, and limbs are blue-black. Her hinged undershell, or plastron, is yellow with black splotches. The hinge is a curious device that allows the turtle to close the front half of its shell slightly in order to better protect its soft fleshy head, neck, and legs from predators.

She may be anywhere from fifteen to twenty years old—the age at which Blanding's turtles reach sexual maturity. Sometime in the spring the Blanding's turtle mated in the lake, she then basked in the sun with her head and legs fully extended. This activity, named thermoregulation by scientists, is thought to help encourage eggs to develop faster.

I crouch on the ground for a closer look. The turtle hisses a warning and ducks her head inside her shell. She patiently waits for me to disappear. I retreat to the porch and watch her with binoculars as she ambles toward the woods to find a soft, sandy place to hollow out a nest with her hind feet. Late that afternoon, almost at dusk, she lays a dozen elliptical white eggs and buries them. Then the forgetful mother ambles away back to the lake.

For the newly laid eggs, the first twenty-four hours will be crucial; often during this time raccoons and skunks ransack the turtle nests. If all goes well, the dark gray hatchlings will emerge in two months, sometime before the first frost. Only as long as my little finger, the hatchlings will have to find their way back to the lake—if they can manage to avoid hungry skunks and raccoons. The lucky ones will reenter the lake and feast on crayfish. They'll be on their own to learn to dive and hide underwater for as long as thirty minutes at a stretch. When the weather turns cool, they'll swim down to the bottom of the lake and bury themselves in the mud to hibernate through the winter.

There's no way to interview the Blanding's turtle or the sandhill crane, who have lived here so many years longer than we have. There is no possibility of reading the recorded days of countless early Paleo-indians who killed mastodons here and, later, the various Potawatomi, Ho-Chunk, and Menominee tribes who may have camped among these oak openings on the nearby hills. These are silent voices.

The earliest written records that exist about this place come from white settlers, who arrived in the 1830s and found the wetland detestable, something to avoid. They skirted this miry place with a kind of terror and loathing, They seldom lingered here or chose this spot to settle on and build, so afraid were they of miasmas and the shakes, the mosquitoes and the axle-breaking mud. To them, there was little beauty in the wetland—only waste. For many European settlers, the marsh was a place that could not be plowed, a place where no cattle could safely graze, a place that no one would dare build a house or barn on without it sinking from sight.

Deputy Surveyor John Brink and his three assistants undoubtedly possessed many of the nineteenth century's prejudices against wetlands when they arrived in Michigan Territory—what would one day be southeastern Wisconsin—in late fall, 1835. The ground at that time of year was still soft and treacherous enough to suck off a man's boots.

There were no houses, no roads, no bridges. The closest settlement—a dozen families huddled along Lake Michigan—was three-days' walk away. Brink and his men traveled mostly on foot, carrying everything they needed on their backs: tent, wool blankets, some hardtack crackers and salt pork, heavy surveying equipment, and precious compass. They had one gun for game hunting— scarcely an adequate weapon to defend the entire expedition from wild beasts or hordes of "Black Hawk savages" they may have feared still lurked in the woods or marshes.

During their rigorous journey that might last five to eleven months, Brink and his two chainmen, ax man, cook, and pack-man were setting up new camps nearly every other day. Sometimes they used logs to build a cache or protected enclosure for their supplies in order to lessen their load. "One had to be an experienced woodsman to do this work," Brink later wrote.

Staying dry was almost impossible. "I have wandered through miles of swamp and on more than one occasion have had to swim streams when ice was running," Brink recalled. "I have been three months at one time without all my clothes dry on me at one time." There was no time to sit around a campfire to dry their clothing. Carrying extra suits was out of the question when they were trying to travel light.

Horse-pulled wagons would not have been much use in marshy places where they became easily sloughed—mired and stuck fast. So far from civilization, there was little hope of rescue. "We did not see much of fashionable society," wrote Brink with a touch of sardonic humor—perhaps a commentary on their filthy condition. "Though we did attend a wedding but were never given the opportunity to kiss the bride."

In spite of deep mud, Brink and his crew plunged ahead single-file across this wetland. They walked an invisible line north-south, then east-west.

Knee-deep in swamp mud, two of Brink's assistants hauled a four-pole, sixty-six-foot chain. One chain man followed the other, measuring the half-mile Brink directed so that the axe man (the third member of the crew) could mark the corners. The chain man in the lead carried eleven metal pins tied at the top with red cloth. He marked the taut chain length with these pins. When he reached the eleventh pin, he called, "Tally!" The second chain man collected the pins and counted them and the process began again. A half-mile was marked with four tallies. The third assistant carried an axe to blaze trees and set corner posts—all signs that would be later used to identify the starting and ending points of imaginary boundaries.

Part of what Brink and his crew surveyed would be called Section 13. One square mile. Fold Section 13 in half and then in half again. Examine just one square—the one in the upper left hand corner. Exactly 160 acres. A tiny thumbprint really. Half water, mostly grass, reeds, a few shrubs and up on the hills, stands of bur oak. This low flat marshy place that encompassed three-springs, a thirty-acre lake, a winding stream, and not much solid ground.

As a surveyor, Brink was not expected to poetically record his findings. He got his job strictly from political connections. Among the job requirements was legible handwriting so that "field notes . . . form a full and perfect history of your operations in the field." "The language of your field notes," wrote Surveyor General Robert Lytle in Cincinnati, "must be so concise and clear, the hand in which they are written so plain and legible, that no doubt can exist as to your figures, letters, words or meaning."

All rivers, creeks and other streams, lakes, ponds, prairies, swamps, marshes, groves, hills, bluffs, windfalls, road and trails were to be distinguished in his full field notes by their original and received names, only. "Where such names cannot be ascertained or do not exist," warned Lytle, "your imagination is not to supply them."

At the same time, Brink's orders were to hurry. Land sales were to begin the following year. "[T]he surveys should be completed at the earliest day possible," wrote Lytle, "in order to meet the requirements of the immigration that [will soon] surge into eastern Wisconsin."

Brink and his assistants undoubtedly discovered how humbling it could be to too hastily cross a marsh on foot. Solid ground gave way at any moment. The surveying crew floundered in mud and ooze. Their experience was undoubtedly similar to that of a Michigan surveyor, who wrote in 1833, "While surveying this day we were most of the time waist deep in water."

A marsh was not a comfortable place for humans. Unlike water fowl and other marsh inhabitants, humans have nothing about their anatomy that's designed to cope with unpredictable ground conditions. Human legs are not long enough to wade through water. Their feet are not broad enough to snow-shoe across mud flats or narrow and clinging enough to clutch branches. Without wings or gills or perching claws, Brink and his men were in trouble trying to cross the swamp.

As another surveyor, Harry Wiltse, recalled after surveying a Wisconsin swamp in 1847, "during the four consecutive weeks, there was not a dry garment in the party day or night." Brink's records from other swampy regions echo Wiltse's complaints: "marsh . . . miry . . . impassable." Most of the time the surveyors were hungry, wet, cold, tired, and badly bitten by mosquitoes and deer flies.

The best thing to do, surveyors like Brink and Wiltse agreed, was to get in and get out of a marsh as fast as possible. After all, who would know whether you actually traversed the land that was so mosquito-infested, quaking, and miry? Brink scribbled something in his book. He looked around Section 13 and scribbled some more: "Land rolling second rate. Burr oak and black oak. Red root rosinweed and cypress."

He called most of what he saw "wet prairie" and kept slogging through the wetness, not bothering to note how the tall stands of dried cattails and bulrush rattled in the cool wind. He failed to record how red-winged blackbirds fed on wild rice or how numberless ducks and geese covered the open waters. He forgot to mention the color of the sky or how the wind smelled or the way the tall rushes whistled and bent over.

Deputy Surveyor Brink was in such a hurry, he didn't bother to meander, or survey, the small lake nearby. He didn't bother walking around to carefully measure the unimpressive, mitten-shaped lake. Maybe it was too puny. Just thirty acres. And his boss had said, "Meander anything more than forty acres."

Brink never wrote the lake up in his notes. He drew a small, half-hearted circle beside the larger lake he sketched hastily in his personal notes, a kind of hurried after thought that never made in official reports to his boss in Cincinnati.

And that was this wetland's first bit of luck.

According to maps made a year later in Cincinnati from Brink's notes, the lake did not exist. Other lakes, clustered in groups like schools of fish, were included in early maps of the area—compete with diagrams of islands and depths of shoreline.

Not this one.

Spidery scrawl marked each plat map section, identified by perfectly straight dividing lines. And so by some strange twist of fate, Section 13 was *not* unlucky, rather, it became the name for a place with remarkable good fortune. The land was simply marked "swamp"—a kind of menace, a hindrance, a malarial wasteland, according to most prospective buyers. A place to be avoided at all cost.

And that was this wetland's second piece of good luck.

## July

Heat cooks the marsh, cloaks it in a tight embrace. I drag the kayak down the path through the crowded rushes and reeds. The path is perilous and slippery with thick black mire. To wear the swamplike clothing in summer means my feet are wet, mud tries to suck away my boots, mosquitoes buzz in my ears, the smell of mud shifts in my nostrils, sharp tendrils of rice cutgrass tug my arms, reeds poke me in the face. Life boils over from hidden, unexpected places.

Yet so much is out of sight. Cattails crowd the water's edge, green and sinewy. Animals, birds, insects are concealed by sedges and vertical formations. Everything alive seems to be racing. The air is noisy as a crowded city street: geese honk, mosquitoes whine, redwings shout, "Where are you?"

"Over here!" another answers.

Reeds hit me in the face, mosquitoes whine in my ears. I am hungry to find something. I try too hard. Drop the paddle and have to return up the path again to find it. On my way I discover a small brown toad nearly, as imperceptible as a clod of dirt. He sits beside the paddle. I would have missed this. I need to slow down and watch more carefully.

I push the front half of the kayak into the water, step inside, and carefully lower myself in with my camera. I slip off my hot rubber boots, tuck them in the front of the kayak. Barefoot is the only way to travel now.

I push up my sleeves, adjust my wide-brimmed hat. Then I shove off with great effort through the soupy mud. The white water lilies are so thick I have to pole my way with great effort. The blossoms whisper loud and insistent beneath the bottom of the kayak. A scritching, scratching sound that warns any heron around the bend to flee before I approach. There is no way to move quietly through the stream in midsummer.

Profusion of lilies in mid-summer. I pause and listen. Suddenly something hidden among the tangled green of floating plants whacks the bottom of the kayak with a vigorous thump. A muscular carp that seems as big as Moby Dick thrashes out of sight. The sound startles languorous painted turtles sunning themselves in stacks. The turtle pile slips, collapses, and with stubby legs flailing they scramble into the water.

I dip my finger into the current. It feels strangely tepid, yet cooler than the air. Haze hangs over the marsh and heat enfolds me. I drift.

A great blue heron stands in the tall reeds, immobile, watching me. *Qaaaaa-aaaark!* It calls in a grating cry. The elegant-looking bird with the ugly voice crouches, extends its gray, six-foot wingspan, takes off, and lands on another tussock. I follow.

So suspicious and cautious, the great blue heron is a solitary wader that's been nicknamed Blue Cranky, Poor Joe, and Long John. These seem fitting titles for such a tall skinny bird that appears to be almost entirely long thin neck, long black legs, and long sharp beak.

A profusion of lilies in mid-summer.

From tip of its beak to its toes, the heron measures almost four feet yet it weighs only six or eight pounds. Perfectly adapted for the wetland, the heron has three-toed, webbed feet that act like snowshoes to keep the bird from sinking into the mud.

As I watch, the heron lifts one long black leg slowly as to not ripple the water and alarm the unsuspecting fish. With one toe the heron carefully stirs the calm surface so that swirling reflections of light make it easier for it to see its target. The heron's job is to concentrate and stand perfectly still. Gifted with keen eyesight, the heron can shift its perception from telescopic to macroscopic in a matter of seconds in order to spot underwater prey. The heron's eyes are located toward the back of its head, which gives it the ability to search nearly 360 degrees in all directions. The heron's strange eye placement, however, may be what gives it such an aloof look.

When mating season arrives in spring, the great blue heron male sports two long, slender black plumes on the back of its head. These jaunty feathers were nearly the heron's undoing one hundred years ago, when the bird was hunted nearly to extinction. Great blue heron plumes were the rage on fashionable ladies' hats at the turn of the century.

I watch as the heron poises its beak above the water. What's happening down there? Perhaps a small, unwary fish is swimming nearby. With a sharp jab, the heron makes a stab. It flips the fish into the air, swallows it headfirst. With an enormous flap, the heron heads skyward with its head pulled back and its neck in an S-shape.

### After the Surveyors

Before the ink was dry on the survey maps, the rush for land began in the southeastern region of Wisconsin, which was still part of Michigan Territory. Not surprisingly perhaps, the very first claim was made by surveyor John Brink and his two assistants, the Ostrander brothers. In October 1835 Brink and Reuben T. and William Ostrander hurried to the Milwaukee land office to claim Section 36 near the outlet of Lake Geneva—a perfect place to set up a water-powered mill. Unfortunately for their dreams of easy wealth, their claim was deemed invalid.

Early 1836 marked the beginning of the trickle of settlers. On July 3, 1836, Wisconsin Territory was created. Soon the arrivals became a flood, fueled in part by Eastern newspapers that had covered Chief Black Hawk's 1832 defeat in lurid detail and now declared that the Wisconsin Territory was officially emptied of all "dangerous savages." Few editors seemed interested in reporting that a few straggling Indians wandered from enforced exile in Iowa back across the Mississippi to their homeland to hide and hunt in Wisconsin marshes—places they knew invading settlers would avoid.

Land selling for $1.25 per acre created a frenzy of speculation. "Land is a drug everywhere," reflected a British visitor to southeastern Wisconsin in 1841. "But water, and water power, has a mystic charm that draws men together in this country."

In 1837 only 200 people were recorded in a crude southeastern Wisconsin census of what would one day be known as Walworth County. Just eleven months later, that number leapt to 1,019. By 1840 the county population had more than doubled to 2,611. Two years later the count had nearly doubled again, this time to 4,618.

The first wave of settlers came on Great Lake sloops and steamboats, by wagon, on horseback, and on foot—mostly from New York, Pennsylvania, Connecticut, Ohio, Michigan, Vermont, and

Massachusetts. They were an assemblage of American-born carpenters, ministers, ne'er do wells, merchants, mama's boys, lawyers, land sharks, farmers, and thieves. Some came alone. Some came with bachelor friends from the old neighborhood. There were those who brought their families and others who set up claims and then sent for their wives and children. Many intended to sink their roots in the territory by farming and making improvements on the land. Others were on the lookout for an easy buck, a sure bet. Like so many other American dreamers, they intended to buy land cheaply, sell it for a handsome profit, and move on to the next real-estate opportunity.

Wide open country with few trees—except for oak openings—impressed many early visitors to the region. "You may ride your horse or in your waggon [*sic*] a hundred miles in any direction without reaching an obstruction," wrote sixty-one-year-old Platt S. Beach of Walworth County in a letter home to his New York relatives in 1846.

Each traveler saw a different landscape when he or she arrived. A settler's age, responsibilities, experience, and previous environments colored perceptions. Former British navy captain Frederick Marryat journeyed across southern Wisconsin Territory in 1837. The rolling country reminded him of a "long swell of the ocean." Ridges and hills between these "gentle undulating flats" were covered with large oaks, spread far enough apart that "you could gallop your horse through any part of it." Marryat, forty-five, compared these oak openings to "English park scenery."

Platt S. Beach, who grew up in upstate New York among fruit trees, claimed the oak openings "have an appearance of an old orchard of fifty years standing with a green sward beneath them." Impressionable and romantic nineteen-year-old Frederick J. Starin of Montgomery County, New York, declared the openings were the "oak orchard of the wild man where the wood-pigeon fluttered unharmed."

To Starin, Wisconsin was nothing short of Eden. After experiencing a spectacular May morning in 1840 exploring a small lake only two miles from where I live, Starin recorded his impressions. In exquisite penmanship, he described in his diary a "mirrored lake where the loon, Duck, pickerel in safety revelled, strangers to the fear and persecution of the civilized man. . . . All was harmony, natural, varied & matchless enchantment."

Recorded enthusiasm for wetlands, or sloughs, however, never matched this kind of breathless wonder. Wetlands were generally viewed by settlers and travelers as hindrances at best and dangers at worst. In 1836 there were no roads. Travelers followed the network of ancient Indian trails that had been worn six to ten inches deep along ridges to connect Indian villages, rivers, and prime hunting and fishing areas—namely wetlands, rivers, and lakes.

If settlers veered off well-marked pathways during spring or summer, they were certain to be sloughed, stuck in a marsh's deep mud with a broken wheel axle or worse. Heavily loaded wagons and carriages pulled by teams of horses or oxen rarely traveled far without some wetland catastrophe.

Charles M. Baker, his wife, and their children had already moved numerous times before they came to Wisconsin Territory. Baker had failed at a variety of occupations—bartender, teacher, merchant, lawyer—in Montreal, Canada, and towns in New York, Vermont, and Pennsylvania. In the winter of 1837, he paid what debts he could, "having made up his mind," he said, "to seek my fortune in the great West."

In September 1838, with only $164 to pay his travel expenses and buy land, Baker packed up his belongings and boarded a Great Lakes steamboat for Detroit with his pregnant wife and three children under age seven. After they arrived, they made the rest of the way by wagon overland to Chicago. Their goods somehow did not come with the steamboat. The family ended up spending the winter in Lake Geneva in an abandoned cabin with no floor, a leaking roof, and a broken door. The furniture consisted of one old chair. Luckily, their neighbors generously shared furniture and bedding.

In June 1839 it took Baker nearly a week to travel a little over fifty miles through numerous marshes from Lake Geneva to Milwaukee to retrieve his household goods that had finally arrived via steamer. He drove three ox teams and two lumber wagons "in which we did battle with the stumps and log bridges . . . got 'sloughed' on the prairies, pried out wagons numerous times, forded streams, broke wagon tongues" and had to build new ones with hickory trees.

In the summer of 1838, Bishop Jackson Kemper, a remarkably proper Episcopal missionary who never went anywhere without an umbrella, traveled up the Mississippi from St. Louis, then crossed southern Wisconsin by foot and by wagon. A squeamish traveler, he constantly complained in his diary of bad food, uncouth settlers, and filthy places to stay. One of his most deplorable accommodations, he wrote, was a dilapidated cabin "visited by a toad and a howling dog beneath the floorboards."

On July 30, 1838, near Duck Creek, while trying to cross a so-called swamp with a horse and carriage, the bishop and his companions decided to make the crossing using a crude walkway someone had laid out with logs. Immediately, they fell into the muck. The mired horses had to be coaxed to safety. The carriage was laboriously pulled over the logs by hand. "We drew near the end of our journey when another very bad place occurred," he wrote. Again, both of the horses floundered haunch deep in marsh mud. One companion fell "up to his middle in the water."

The trip proved to be a true test of the bishop's Christian patience. The next morning after a fresh start, "one of our horses fell crossing a swamp place." On August 3 he reported with vexation, "Much swamp—deep holes—steep hills." The only way they could get the carriage down the hills was to lower it with ropes.

Starin, who was younger, fitter, and a less finicky eater, recorded a slightly different impression of sloughs. In late May 1840 the temperature became unseasonably hot as he hiked north from what's now called Lake Geneva. "Brook after brook & slough after slough did I wade," he wrote in his diary. "Bluff after bluff did I thus ascend but not a tree, nor house nor fence nor object of any kind was there to catch my wearied eye all was once waste of weeds and grass."

On another warm morning in May, Starin made an eight-mile hike to what's now Cold Spring, Jefferson County. He described the route as "alternately over bluff openings and very wet marshes, succeeding each other at regular intervals." He slogged in ankle-deep water for half a mile across a marsh to a small, shallow stream he called the Bark River. "The south bank is dry & much resembles the Mohawk Flatts," Starin wrote, comparing the spot with an upstate New York landmark. "Here also grow wild onions in abundance. The north is very low & wet & covered with high grass."

Gallantly, Starin picked a bunch of wild onions and brought them home to his host, who served them with vinegar. That evening two of his host's sons gave a violin concert. Somehow it seems fitting to think of young Starin happily munching away on wetland onions with a Mendelssohn duet playing in the background.

Another young man, East Coast theology school graduate Solomon Ashley Dwinnell, wandered into Walworth County in 1836. The twenty-four-year-old was frail and stoop-shouldered—not a promising pioneer candidate. And yet he seemed to have had few bad first experiences with local marshes—or at least none that he later remembered. When he jotted down his earliest memories of this place, he noted in a positive tone that west of Honey Creek was "an extensive wet prairie and marsh . . . which offered the early settlers a fine chance to cut hay for wintering their stock."

Sedge or "marsh hay" that grew in the wetlands in August were a boon for early settlers. The soft, wiry plants made good cattle feed and bedding. Years later marsh hay would be used as packing for huge chunks of ice harvested from small nearby lakes in winter and stored in cavernous barns. The ice was hauled to Milwaukee, where it was used for transporting beer by train to Chicago.

Besides bottomless mud, another common complaint about wetlands among pioneer travelers during the warm months was the presence of dense swarms of insects. Black flies tormented cattle until they were nearly driven mad. "Clouds of mosquitoes infested the openings and drove sleep and slumber from the settlements," recalled one resident of Walworth County.

Throughout the summer of 1838 Bishop Kemper and his traveling companions were plagued by vicious mosquitoes. Nothing seemed to keep the biting bugs away—neither smoky fires nor mosquito nets. In one camp with "no water, no wood, and plenty of mosquitoes," Kemper wrote in his diary how he tried unsuccessfully to sleep sitting up in the carriage with his coat buttoned, mosquito net over his face, and leather gloves on his hands.

Many travelers and settlers feared "swamp miasmas," vapors that reportedly floated up from wetlands at night and were believed to cause illness. Platt S. Beach reassured his relatives not to worry. He had purchased 160 acres for $750 in Walworth County. "Our situation is commanding for this level country," he bragged. "No marsh within a mile of us, and if there is any pure air in Wisconsin, or in the world, we inhale it."

Settlers blamed what they called "gaseous emissions arising from stagnant water" in marshes for "swamp fever" or ague, a tenacious, widespread malady that hit hard in southeastern Wisconsin and other Midwestern settlements in the nineteenth century. "It seemed to descend upon the country like a blanket," wrote Dr. Isaac Stephenson, a physician who settled in southeastern Wisconsin Territory in the early 1840s. For five years he was afflicted by the disease, which became so severe at one point he had to stop practicing medicine.

"Even the dogs shook in the spring and autumn," proclaimed one early folk saying about "ague-and-chill fever." Men, women, and children who succumbed to the disease sometimes trembled with a terrific chill. Other times they burned with fever. The illness came on suddenly, went away, then returned without warning. Victims were often so weakened they could not get out of bed or work—a disastrous situation for first-year settler families who depended on adults' ability to perform physical labor necessary for survival.

"Commenced shaking today," noted one settler over and over again in his diary of 1840. The disease, although not life-threatening, was so common nearly everyone was afflicted at some point. "He ain't sick," went one saying, "he only got the ague."

Swamp gas was blamed; so were plowing "wild soil," drought, too much horseback riding, and eating too many melons. One early resident who claimed marshes did *not* cause disease was Increase A. Lapham. He insisted that Wisconsin was one of the most healthy places in the world. "Wet meadows, marshes, and swamps," he wrote in his 1846 Wisconsin guide book for prospective settlers, "are constantly supplied with pure water from springs; and as they are not exposed during summer to burning heat, they do not send forth those noxious and deleterious qualities so much dreaded in more southern and less favored latitudes."

However, no other writer at the time did as much to promote negative stereotypes about Midwestern wetlands as Charles Dickens. In 1842 he published his widely circulated observations about a trip through the Midwest. Everything about what Dickens saw, heard,

Early morning mist floats eerily over the fen.

and smelled appalled him. He despised the croaking sound of frogs, the "rank unseemly growth, the unwholesome steaming earth . . . the stagnant, slimy, rotten, filthy water."

Dickens's painfully slow travel in carriage and horse through axle-deep mud did nothing to improve his humor. How could people possibly choose to live here, he fumed? A wetland was nothing less than "a hotbed of disease, an ugly sepulchre, a grave uncheered by any gleam of promise: a place without one single quality, in earth or air or water to commend it."

Not until 1900 did scientists prove that ague was a form of malaria, a disease carried by a specific mosquito that was brought over on sailing ships. The female mosquito, which breeds in stagnant water—not just wetlands but any standing puddle—lays its eggs at night on the surface of the water after it has had a meal of blood. The female gathers the blood by biting any human or animal when the temperature is sixty-two degrees Fahrenheit or warmer. Malarial parasites inside the mosquito's stomach are passed into a human's bloodstream and end up in the liver. Meanwhile, the mosquito's jet black, cylindrical eggs hatch in two days—creating another cycle of mosquitoes eagerly gobbled up by many wetland birds, reptiles, and amphibians.

Quinine was not discovered as a way to treat ague until 1880s. Some settlers used dubious cures, such as "Dr. Mowl's Medicine." Meanwhile, during warm months, mosquitoes continued to plague settlers—in spite of smoky smudge fires. Affordable window screens had not been invented. In the 1840s very few of the early Wisconsin log cabins had "more than six panes of eight-by-ten glass, to let sunlight in upon their inmates," according to the *History of Walworth County* published in 1882.

More deadly for early Wisconsin settlers than ague, however, were diseases like Asiatic cholera, which hit in 1854 and typhoid, which ran through entire families and communities with terrifying speed. Little did anyone at the time realize that these diseases were caused by water supplies that were contaminated when surrounding wetlands were treated as garbage dumps and places to discard outhouse refuse.

In 1842 Edwin Bottomley, a woolen mill worker from England, came to America with his wife and children to acquire a thirty-five-acre tract in an English settlement in western Racine County, where he built a brick house for his growing family. He wrote copious letters to his father in England during the eight years of his life in Wisconsin Territory, describing everything from what he planted in his vegetable garden to the trials of starting and building a church. As his family grew, so did the surrounding community.

In June 1844 he wrote that his nearest water supply was nearly half a mile away. "We fetch our water from it that we Drink it is about as strong a spring as *old Moll* and comes out of an hillside the other springs rise on the marshy land and are not as good." He seldom complained of marsh miasma.

Six years later, however, the entire Bottomley family was ravaged by typhoid fever in the autumn of 1850. Three of the five children and both parents came down the disease. Forty-one year old Edwin died in November, leaving his children and widow in considerable debt. Sadly, a few weeks later his newborn granddaughter also died.

## Snake Stories and Tales of Other Disappearing Wetland Animals

As the settler population in southeastern Wisconsin flourished, early wetland animal populations declined. One of the first casualties was the Eastern Massasauga rattlesnake, whose name comes from the Chippewa language and means "great river mouth." Believed erroneously by many early settlers to be a dangerous wetland serpent, the massasauga was diligently eliminated wherever encountered. In 1835 one zealous southeastern Wisconsin farmer reportedly killed thirty-five one day while plowing. During the summer of 1836 another Walworth County settler reportedly killed seven snakes in one afternoon.

This relatively small rattlesnake, ranging from twenty-four to thirty-seven inches in length, resided in wetlands on a diet of small birds and reptiles. The tan snake with blackish blotches didn't always use a warning rattle, whose sound has been compared to a ticking watch, to indicate its anger.

Contrary to popular wisdom, the massasauga produces a limited amount of venom, which is not usually fatal. Settlers who were bitten used poultices of wood ashes and large doses of whisky as antidotes. Indians reportedly rubbed their bodies with dried, powdered turkey-buzzard flesh as a cure.

By 1850, rattlesnakes had disappeared—wiped out by frenzied, armed settlers and their hogs. Hogs ran wild in unfenced woods, meadows, and wetlands and attacked snakes wherever they found them. From the stories told about hogs, one would think they were second only to their owners in their zeal to wipe out massasaugas.

Rattlesnakes were not the only animals that quickly disappeared from the southeastern Wisconsin landscape with the rising tide of settlers; by 1840 elk were extinct. The only reminders of the great herds were antlers found in streambeds and marshes or embedded in oak trees. White-tailed deer that abounded in woods and drank from lakes in 1838 were overhunted so severely that the last deer was killed near Delavan by 1846.

Black bears, which ate so plentifully from fallen acorns in oak openings, helped give the bur oak the nickname "bear acorn." In the summer bears ventured into swamps to eat berries. By 1836 the last black bear in Walworth County had been shot. Flocks of wild turkeys commonly roamed woods and meadows in the area until 1846, when a series of severe winters and overhunting collapsed the population, and the last turkey was killed near Racine. Sandhill cranes, which were commonly seen in wetlands and prairies became rarer and rare by 1850, partially because they were hunted for food and partially because their habitat was being restricted or drained.

In 1845 an observer reported that Honey Creek was "full of fish and lakes and streams were alive with muskrats, minks and otter." Because of its valuable fur, the otter was trapped extensively in lakes and wetlands. In 1835 4,831 pelts were collected in La Pointe, Wisconsin. By the time of Wisconsin statehood in 1848, the number of otter pelts collected dropped to 321.

## Thunderstorms and Oak Trees

In the midday torpor, all becomes quiet. A lone cloud skims overhead. Birds, hidden, call to one another. Sun dapples shadows of glistening leaves. It's too hot, too hazy for anything to move except for dragonflies and midges. Scum floats on the water. Waterstriders wheel and skate across the surface. Even turtles hide from this much sunshine. A kind of sleep overtakes them—almost as if they've entered the extreme of winter's cold again.

That afternoon while I paddle in the kayak on the lake, I hear a thunderstorm crash and rumble in the distance. The sky to the west bruises purple. Suddenly, lightning stabs the horizon. I paddle as fast as I can to retreat from the water. Later, I learn that a giant oak tree in my neighbor's front yard was struck by lightning. A stout branch sheared away and crashed to the road, just missing their roof.

The power and unpredictability of summer thunderstorms makes me think about the experience of first-year settlers. Living out in the open when there were so few trees must have meant that the sky, the thunder, the lightning had even more enormous dimensions. Lightning was often the agent of another ever-present phenomenon in spring and fall: fire.

Few early settlers realized that the oak openings, or natural parks, they admired so much were often the result of lightning strikes that sparked fires which raced across the landscape. The bur oak was one tree that could withstand the flames that destroyed shrubs and other tree competitors. Even as the first settlers began to appear in the county, fires were still a very present danger.

Late-summer thunderstorms and accompanying lightning were terrifying for many early settlers. One woman, who grew up in Jefferson County and later farmed near Whitewater, recalled, "While alone with my young boys, I spent much time gazing heavenward for the speck of cloud in the distance, which with the fierce gale and the first roar of thunder announced that the storm was upon us."

The sound was deafening. "Twenty four-pounders cannot exceed the crash and roar of a Wisconsin thunderstorm," wrote Platt S. Beach, who blamed the frequency and violence of storms on the "mineral region" and the presence of so many oak trees, which were, he said, "electrifying." There is some credence to the folklore that claims oak trees attract lightning.

According to one naturalist, mineral-laden moisture carried specifically in oak tree cells from the roots to top branches is actually a perfect conductor for electrical energy—a kind of "pathway from the raised branches to the buried roots." The high temperatures that are generated by a huge electrical surge can actually cause wood fibers to explode. A German forester a century ago studied fifty thousand acres of trees and found that an oak tree's high water content makes it sixty times more likely to be struck by lightning than a beech tree, which has much oilier wood.

My neighbor's ancient oak has a large taproot and a few vertical ancillary roots, but it remains standing because of a broad horizontal root system. This means that oaks are particularly dangerous trees for humans or animals to hide beneath during electrical storms. And yet it makes me wonder if perhaps the old folk adage that oak trees attract lightning may somehow reflect an interesting relationship: Did bur oaks attract lightning as a means of self-preservation for their tree species? Lightning created large-scale fires that once kept fireproof oak trees dominant here. Was oak self-immolation a form of sacrifice for the larger good?

I wish I could ask a tree the answer to this question.

Early settlers recalled that fires were more frequent in autumn after the dieback of prairie grasses and wetland sedges and cattails. "The least spark of fire, or the flash of a gun, [the mat of dead grass] will all in blaze," wrote Platt S. Beach, who noted that prairie grass grew two feet tall before it withered. "By this blaze the horizon is lighted up throughout the fall and winter in all directions."

Earlier that spring in the evening he noticed smoke rising on the horizon. "The whole world," he wrote, "appeared to be in a blaze. Night became as day and thousands of acres appeared to be one mass of liquid burning lava."

Six years earlier, in October 1840, Frederick J. Starin recorded in his diary what he saw near Waukesha: "Very hard west wind, clear. This evening I saw five fires burning in different directions." A week later in Mukwanago he noted: "Fires Burned down between the two branches of White Water to-day." The next day the fire had spread. "White Water Prairie burned this P.M.," he wrote, adding laconically in his next entry. "Burnt Stack." The terror of being caught in a fire was something only Platt admitted: "The scene was grand and sublime—even to the terrible."

Just as the prairies burned, so did the sedge meadows and wetlands. Rivers, streams, and lakes, surrounded by wetlands, were often where fires were slowed or eventually stopped—depending on wind speed and direction. The fire kept in check the spread of low shrubs in the sedge meadow to regenerate new, thicker growth, thus improving grazing. When Platt described the burning horizon as "grand and sublime," he was viewing sedge meadows and wetlands on fire as well.

Every passing year fires lessened in impact and frequency. More plowed fields, more roads, more people to put out accidental fires meant that slowly the landscape was beginning to change. Shrubs and small trees sprang up in oak openings. Trees like elm, ash, and cottonwood began to grow where none had ever thrived before. Red osier dogwood and other nonnative shrubs, including buckthorn and honey suckle, slowly took hold on the edges of sedge meadows that weren't cut for hay or used as pasture. Fire, which had been a tool for control used by Indians, was now being replaced by the plow, the ax, and the cow.

## Land Records, Mud, and Silent Stones

When news of a California gold strike crowded newspaper headlines across the country in the spring of 1848, William Wheeler did not head west in search of a lucky strike in the Sacramento Valley. Instead he took another kind of gamble. He bought forty acres of wet meadow and swamp in Section 13 in the newly formed state of Wisconsin.

Wheeler was an unlikely risk-taker. While the majority of the new state's population were young, single men, according to the 1850 census, fifty-two-year-old Wheeler had a wife and three school-aged daughters, ranging in age from eight to thirteen. A Wisconsin Territory resident since 1842, Wheeler was one of a large wave of "Yankee-Yorkers" who migrated from upstate New York via the Erie Canal and the Great Lakes. In the 1850 census he would list his occupation as "farmer."

There is no record describing what circumstances propelled Wheeler to saddle his horse and make the fateful forty-one-mile journey along muddy, nearly impassable roads from Troy to Milwaukee. The city bustled with German-speaking immigrants who had just disembarked from steamboats anchored in Milwaukee's harbor. The area near North Pier thronged with strange languages and garb; the smells of unfamiliar foods; and the ever-present shouting of persistent runners, hotel promoters.

When a steamboat anchored, as many as eight-hundred weary, confused immigrants poured from the hold with all their worldly belongings. In 1847, nearly one-third came from Germany. They funneled into Milwaukee and beyond to escape from crop failure and famine, industrialization and unemployment, revolution, and political disorder. "I have seen hundreds in a vacant lot bargaining for cattle and wagons with which to begin life and establish a farm," wrote Isaac Stephenson, who arrived in Milwaukee in 1845.

After the voters' approval of the constitution ten days before Wheeler's arrival in Milwaukee, Wisconsin had become the thirtieth state. Anything seemed possible, the sky the limit. Milwaukee reflected a kind of enthusiastic hopefulness; it was a city on the make, a place full of contradictions. On some streets could be heard lively debate among newly arrived German intellectual exiles. In other locations, where the plank road had washed away in spring rains, entire teams of oxen disappeared into gaping slough holes. Milwaukee had laws against roving pigs and prudish prohibitions against bathing in the river. At the same time, the city had open sewers, the area around which was called "the Swamp," the poorest of newly arrived immigrants huddled in shanties. It's not surprising, perhaps, that no one had yet agreed how to spell the city's name: Was it "Milwaukee" or "Milwaukie"?

When Wheeler arrived, Milwaukee had already gone through the throes of a boom, bust, and boom cycle so frenzied that at one point a contemporary described the whole place as "an unenclosed lunatic asylum." In the 1830s city lots had changed hands as often as two or three times in a single day. Milwaukee grew in ten years from a straggling fur company settlement beside a sprawling marsh in to a city of more than fifteen thousand in 1848. Milwaukee boasted of a dozen churches, a court house, a bank, and the services of seventeen hundred lawyers.

Land fever gripped everyone—the newly arrived and those who had squatted illegally since the Wisconsin Territory was formed. After a national financial panic and runaway inflation caused by an unsettled national monetary policy, rampant speculation stopped temporarily. And yet, miraculously, the land sale engine restarted again. By 1845, three million acres had already been sold throughout Wisconsin. In one week in 1847, receipts in the land office exceeded $175,000. There seemed no end to the availability of land and how quickly it could be bought and sold again. As Wisconsin's population surged, so did demand and land prices.

For many individuals like Wheeler who were infected by land fever, buying land seemed a sure-fire moneymaker, the best way to get rich quick—in spite of the warnings of such publications as the *Emigrant Handbook and Guide to Wisconsin* that recommended not making a hasty purchase before hiring "a small farm for a season." The handbook cautioned Wisconsin newcomers to "know the quality and eligibility of the land . . . never run into debt with the calculation of paying the purchase money by the produce of the farm." It's debatable whether someone like Wheeler heeded advice such as, "Buy no more land than you can comfortably pay for and after all leave a sufficiency to purchase a few necessaries of life."

On March 23, 1848, William Wheeler elbowed his way into the overheated Milwaukee land office packed with other farmers, merchants, speculators, and money lenders. If he was able to get close enough to examine the plat maps and surveyor notes, he would have seen that most of Section 13 had already been purchased by fellow New Yorkers, with a smattering of purchases by men from Vermont and Connecticut. The best farm land and an oak opening—a forty-acre tract in the far northwest corner—had been purchased nearly six years earlier. In 1846 another 240 acres had disappeared.

What was left when Wheeler made his bid was wetland and crooked stream, sandy hills with a few bur oaks, and treacherous access to the southernmost section of the lake. The only other bidder in Section 13 in 1848 was Nelson Lake, a forty-five-year-old farmer from New York who had a wife, Rebecca, forty-eight, and plenty of help: two sons over age sixteen and three teenage daughters.

At the Milwaukee land office the clerk conducting the land auction sat on a platform and called out the remaining parcels township by township, section by section.

"Section 13, northwest quarter of the southwest quarter," the clerk shouted. "Forty acres."

Wheeler had thirty seconds to make his bid—a minimum of $1.25, or five shillings sterling, per acre—before the clerk moved on to the next parcel. Wheeler raised his hand and indicated fifty dollars—the minimum price for the minimum amount of land allowed in sale.

Silence. No one else bid.

The clerk nodded and made a pen scratch on the list. The land was Wheeler's if he could pay in full. If Wheeler didn't have enough money of his own, he could easily find someone willing to lend him the cash at the outrageous rate of twelve percent or more, payable in installments. The only acceptable form of bank notes at the time was silver or accepted "certificates of deposit" drawn from the Marine and Fire Insurance Company, a peculiar Milwaukee institution that functioned like a bank.

Wheeler paid his money to the federal government, signed his name, and received a receipt from the clerk. In two years he would be sent from Washington, D.C., a copy of the official patent, which begins with Shakespearean eloquence: "To all whom these Presents shall come, Greeting." The document, penned in an elegant hand, was signed by a clerk using the name of the current president, Zachary Taylor. "To William Wheeler and to his heirs and assigns forever," the patent proclaims.

There is something concrete, eternal, and grand in the legal wording—even though William Wheeler and his family would prove to have only an ephemeral relationship with Section 13. Records show that by December 1852, an unsatisfied, or unpaid, mortgage had been made on the property by John Sanford to John Boston. Wheeler and his family weren't able to hold on to the land very long.

Although William Wheeler became the first recorded owner of this part of the wetland, it is his wife Miranda who intrigues me. Legally, she was not a coowner, only an heir should her husband die. According to the Wisconsin constitution, she had no property rights. She could not legally conduct her own business, make contracts, retain her own earnings, or sue or be sued in her own name.

She could not purchase her own land. She could not vote. She had little power to stop her husband from making the purchase. And if he died in debt, it would be her duty to repay his creditors.

I wonder what she thought the first time she saw the wetland that blustery, cold spring in 1848. What did Wheeler's daughters, Helen, Amelia, and Ruth Ann, say when their father showed them the expanse of bleached sedges, rattling dry cattails still bent from winter? The unpredictable Midwestern spring weather did not provide much of an auspicious beginning. Just a month after Wheeler made his fateful purchase, a terrific April snow storm hit. "The wind was so Strong," a farmer from Waterford wrote, "that it Drifted all into heaps." Trees and fences were knocked down and a steamboat ran aground on Lake Michigan near Racine, thirty-five miles away.

According to James Marshall in *Land Fever: Dispossession and Frontier Myth,* for Wheeler and other enthusiastic land owners like him, there was "a serpent in the promised garden." If he did not pay outright with his own cash, he faced regular crippling loan payments. This "riddling debt, a mythical beast—part land speculation, part mortgage and interest, part loan shark" posed special dangers for families with little capital in reserve. In 1850, while still owning the forty acres in Section 13, Wheeler claimed to have real estate amounting to $1,000, not a sizable sum among his neighbors. (Nelson Lake, to the north, claimed twice that amount.)

Numerous costs were involved in setting up a farm: building a cabin, buying needed equipment; erecting an outbuilding; digging a well; purchasing necessary livestock, fencing, and seed. With such high expenses, any mishap could provoke financial disaster. The early 1850s in southeastern Wisconsin saw a series of crop failures described in an 1882 county history as the "pink-eye years"—an expression that referred to farmers' tear-soaked faces. Ague and other debilitating illnesses, accidents, and injuries and outright inexperience managing finances created hardships that often caused families to become dispossessed. One of the prominent features of Racine's weekly newspapers in 1848 and throughout the early 1850s were sheriff sales and liquidation notices.

To climb out from under crushing debt was nearly impossible. While lands were cheap, so was labor. Men working as laborers on farms were paid only eight dollars per month. Girls and women who did general housework for pay received as little as seventy-five cents per week. In 1847 men in Milwaukee cut and stacked wood that had been split by their wives for twenty-five cents per cord.

"Losing the farm" became an expression indicating a kind of perpetual hopelessness, a continual moving on to some other place, some other Land of Begin Again. "The fact that lands were cheap," said early settler Isaac Stephenson, "offered little encouragement in the face of trials and privations and uncertainty of success."

Wheeler's purchase of forty acres that were more than 60 percent wetland was in reality hardly a bargain. He and his family would be lucky to harvest enough marsh hay to feed a few cows. The land had dubious value as pasture, since so much of it posed treacherous footing for cows, sheep, and pigs. There were no hardwood trees to speak of. Wheat, the crop of choice among farmers at the time, could not be grown easily on what little sandy soil was dry enough to plow. What exactly Wheeler did with the land, whether he built a house or barn here, is unknown.

Wheeler's signature adorns this Milwaukee Land Office receipt, showing that he bought forty acres of wetland for fifty dollars.

A gravestone marks the grave of Patience, an early settler.

By 1857, just seven years after he received his patent, Wheeler's name vanished from the official local plat map. The eight other owners—all Wheeler's contemporaries in 1850—also disappeared. Section 13 became the province of five landowners. What became of the original patent owners is a mystery.

In an era of easily available land, restlessness was a contagion. Only 39 percent of those present in 1850 as heads of households in the Milwaukee area could still be found there in the 1860 city directory. There was an enormous out-migration even as there was an ongoing in-migration. And 44 percent of the native-born present in 1850 were still residents in the Milwaukee census of 1860. Among those born in Ireland, almost half had moved on in ten years.

Wheeler disappeared from the local census of 1860. He reappeared in 1870, having moved 120 miles northwest to Sauk County on the Wisconsin River. There he listed himself as "retired farmer" and claimed he owned $3,000 in real estate and $700 in personal wealth. Miranda, now seventy, was keeping house, but her daughters had vanished from the Wheeler household (if they were married and changed their names, their location would be difficult to find in the records). An eleven-year old grandson, born in Wisconsin and whose name the census taker failed to record, was listed living with Miranda and William in New Buffalo.

Sometime during the next ten years, William died. Miranda, according to the 1880 census, was still remarkably alive at age eighty. Listing her occupation as "widowed," she lived in the town of Delton with George and Maria Allen, who may have been her son-in-law and daughter. Maria would have been thirteen on the day the census was taken back in Troy. It's impossible to know for certain if she was a missing daughter—or simply another relative who took in Miranda.

And I begin to ponder what happened to Miranda's daughters. Where did they go? What became of them?

Armed with only a few slim facts—their names, the possible years of their births—I decide to investigate the nearest cemetery in hope of discovering something more about William Wheeler and his family.

The town closest to the Wheelers, named Troy reportedly because of ease of spelling, was established with high hopes in 1836 by Major Jesse Meachum, another New Yorker. Meachum had acquired his military title after a brief, disastrous military stint during the War of 1812. He first appeared in Wisconsin Territory in 1835 from Lodi, Michigan.

In 1836 Wisconsin was in the grip of a land-speculation frenzy. A Milwaukee journalist at the time noted: "Men's hats were crammed with maps of paper towns." Like other get-rich-quick enthusiasts, Meachum bought up land where he believed a thriving town was most likely to grow: at the intersection of the two main roads that led to Milwaukee and Janesville and only a few rods away from Honey Creek. Water power was essential to power a grist mill.

"Meachum's," as the place came to be called by locals, was the major's domain. He was innkeeper, postmaster, and tavern-keeper. In 1839 his establishment featured a menu of one item: pork and beans. Five years later Meachum's grist mill was operational. In 1843 he built a forty-foot-wide, hundred-foot-long-barn, the largest in the county. This was used for dancing, weddings and public gatherings, including meetings of the Claim Association.

The major was one of the founding members of this organization, which protected the rights of bona fide early settlers against interlopers—a vague way of saying that the organization took the law into its own hands to remove interlopers and speculators who could outbid prices for land that had already been settled. The major led one particularly daring outing of the Claim Association in 1839, when armed members of the group attempted to remove a claim-jumper who had barricaded himself inside a shanty with his family. After breaking down the door with a battering ram, Meachum entered the shanty, collared the father-in-law of the claim-jumper, reportedly "the heaviest man in the besieged party." He dragged the big man out of the shanty and "sat down on him." Meanwhile, the rest of the Claim Association overpowered the remaining squatters, threw their household goods outdoors, and tore down the shanty.

In spite of Major Meachum's high hopes, Troy would enjoy only eighteen years of growth and prosperity, from 1838 until 1856. In 1850 the population was a little over 1,000. Ten years later, it reached

1,238—the largest it would be. While the rest of the county was thriving in 1870, Troy's population began to drop. When the railroad bypassed Troy and went somewhere else in 1857, local businesses began to leave. Two financial panics and economic depression after the Civil War "wholly blighted every hope," according to a local historian.

Today Meachum's barn is gone. So is the mill, the school that was once a church, and the stores. Residential houses remain—some improved, others in disrepair. Greenwood Cemetery is perhaps one of the most unchanged places from Troy's past. Hidden on a hill behind a peeling 4-H sign, the cemetery is barely visible from the road. It is surrounded on three sides by the back yards of houses and enclosed with a rusty wire fence secured with a wobbly gate fastened with a hook. The cemetery is mowed and kept orderly by loyal members of the 4-H Club.

I spy no flowers adorning grave markers, some of which are so worn and weathered that they have become nearly indecipherable. A few are cracked, leaning, or toppled. The place has a deceptive peacefulness—the same kind of silence you experience in a library until you open books and begin to read. Cemeteries appear silent until you begin reading the markers. And then the stories begin.

Daniel Hooper, for example, has the largest, most resplendent monument in the cemetery. He managed to live to age seventy-one, quite old for the time. Arrayed around him at a respectful distance are plain markers "Mother," "Father," and "Daughter"—all without individual names. Another member of the same clan, Jamin H. Hooper, has a grave site marked with the star emblem of the Grand Army of the Republic. He served 1861 to 1865 as a sergeant in Company 10, Wisconsin Infantry, during the Civil War. Sadly, beside him is the grave site of his young wife, twenty-two-year-old Elvira, who died May 6, 1863, likely while he was gone to war.

I scribble down name after name, date after date. And I discover none of the Wheeler sisters or their descendants. I keep searching.

Here is Major Meachum's modest gravestone. By the time he died in 1868 at age seventy-seven, his promising village had withered. In the 1860 and 1870 censuses, buildings were boarded up or listed as vacant. Local adventurers full of dreams of glory pulled up stakes in 1849 and went to California to prospect for gold. As land opened for homesteading in Iowa, Dakota, and Oregon Territories, there was always another place on the horizon to make a new beginning. Many of the early names listed as "original settlers" in Troy from the mid-1830s to late 1840s vanished in subsequent years. "It cannot be ascertained where he went," the local county history reported over and over again when describing early land owners as "whereabouts unknown."

In spite of tough times, Major Meachum stayed put. So did his stolid wife, Patience, who was buried beside him. She bore three sons by her first husband, the major's brother. After he died, she married Major Meachum. The major never had any children of his own. Aunt Patience, as she was fondly known by locals, survived him by seven years. She died in 1875, age eighty-one.

The most disturbing gravestone I discover is the oldest one at Greenwood Cemetery. It's dated July 10, 1841, nearly seven years before Wheeler bid on his forty acres of wetland. This single limestone marker is the resting place for two children, fourteen-year old Truman Hibbard and his three-year old sister Sophie. They both died on the same summer day. There is no clue why or how. An accident? An epidemic?

I wander among the gravestones, touched by the precariousness of life more than 150 years ago. Of the twenty-nine individuals buried here, more than half were children age two or younger. Grave markers list very specifically the length of these short lives: "Martha A. d. July 14, 1846, 2 y 15 mos 12 dys." "Helen Louisa Smith d. March 4, 1850 age 2 ys 21 dys" and the unnamed: "Also infant of Caleb A. and Polly Smith born and died Nov. 19, 1849."

And suddenly for me the Greenwood Cemetery is populated not just with the dead but the ghosts of survivors who must have come here to grieve these children's passing. Mothers, fathers, brothers, sisters. How many infants are buried on farms, near the edges of woodlots? How many women died in childbirth?

When I leave the cemetery, I carefully latch the wobbly wire gate. I am intent on finding out what happened that summer day to the two Hibbard children. I soon discover that the clues are few and far between. I cannot verify among the many Hibbards who lived in the area the names of the parents. The children do not appear in any census records. Finally, I discover in the diary of Solomon Dwinnell one tantalizing sentence at the bottom of the page: "First deaths . . . Two children of J. Hibbard one a lad named Truman 14 years old."

That was all he wrote. He did not mention the three-year old sister. He doesn't say what happened or why on that July day in 1841.

And so, like my search for Helen, Amelia, and Ruth Ann Wheeler, I reach a sudden, frustrating dead end.

## Fish Stories

Mosquito eggs, larvae, and full grown adults are an important food source for fish. I have to keep this in mind as I am swatting away clouds of mosquitoes that surround my face as I pull the kayak out to the stream.

One of the endangered fish that lives in the lake feasts on mosquitoes with great relish. The starhead topminnow, only two and one-half inches long, spends most of its life on the surface of the water, where it can find plenty of mosquito larvae. The starhead has a metallic silver spot on the top of its head and handsome stripes along its sides. In late spring or early summer, it laid hundreds of eggs among the dense vegetation along the water's edge.

Another fish that had its start in the wetland is the thin, dark northern pike, which can be four feet four inches long as an adult. The female pike lays her eggs in dense vegetation of the wetland. Once the eggs hatch, the sleek young pike thrash noisily as they hurry out into the nearby lake to prey upon ducklings, mosquitoes and aquatic insects.

All kinds of drama is going on at a minute scale along the surface of the water and just below its depths.

The water strider, a slender, long, dark brown wingless insect about a half-inch long, darts about the surface film of the stream and lake without sinking, feeding on floating mosquito larvae. The adult female water strider, which hibernated last winter under leaves at the water's edge, laid rows of eggs at the water's edge. The hatchlings, called nymphs, mature in five weeks.

The nymphs must be clever and quick to avoid the large, air-breathing diving beetle, which stalks its prey underwater. The beetle swims by, moving its hind legs like oars. Small fish, tadpoles, and insect larvae are favorite foods. By hijacking an air bubble, the beetle floats to the surface. Once its oxygen supply is restored, the beetle dives underwater again with oxygen trapped on the hairs of its body.

## *August*

The heat of midsummer melts ambition. It bridles and burdens me with the sense of slow motion. I can hardly think. The suffocation of not being able to breathe, my head throbbing, my eyes squinting. Sweat pours down my forehead and the inside of my arms. Horseflies attack my ears and tangle my hair. Even a hat doesn't help to avoid these pests' fierce determination.

I long for the coolness of water, submersion in the spring-fed lake. I paddle out in the kayak to the middle of the lake, wiggle out of the seat and lower myself off the bow into the deep, blue-black water. Long reeds wave and tickle my legs. I think of predacious beetles and leeches that nip. The leering, toothy grins of pike flash across my mind. But I'm too hot, too desperate to allow such visions to stop me. I splash and float, my head bobbing among those countless turtles seeking the same escape, the writhing streamlined movement of water snakes and the bending and unbending of kicking frogs.

At last I am cool!

### A Menace and Hindrance

By the middle of the nineteenth century, Congress declared openly what so many Americans had believed for years to be true: swamps were a menace, a hindrance.

Thousands of acres of wetlands throughout the United States were passed over for purchase by settlers and speculators. These lands remained vacant, idle, unwanted. For the federal government, which sold and profited from all public land sales, this was a terrible waste. But what could be done? Wetlands were deemed worthless. Who wanted a soggy piece of "notoriously malarial" land unfit for cultivation?

In September 1850, congressional leaders came up with what seemed at least on paper to be a thoughtful solution: the Swamp Lands Act. The states could decide what sections and parcels were swamp or overflowed land. Sold at a discount, these land sales would go straight back into the state's pocket. This new source of funding would allow states to set up drainage projects. This would cause "great sanitary improvement" and create new, usable acres, Congress argued. Reclamation of swamps would also enhance the value and sale of adjoining property. States had fairly wide jurisdiction about how exactly swamp sale revenue could be used. And that little loophole meant that the Swamp Lands Act began to veer from its original intent.

Lucky for Section 13.

The first hurdle in administering the Swamp Lands Act had to do with choice. States were supposed to decide which parcels were wetland and which weren't. Naturally, no one could agree. Was it land that flooded periodically or land that was always wet? Survey notes weren't always reliable, especially if the surveyor had visited a wetland during a dry season. Local knowledge, "certified by reliable citizens" was often tainted with greed and personal economic interest. Not surprisingly, extensive fraud took place. So-called swamp lands (which was often good land) sold at cut-rate prices of one dollar an acre or less somehow ended up in the wrong hands.

By 1868 the House of Representatives Committee on Public Lands declared that there had been many abuses across the country; nearly half the swamp land act grants had been snatched up by speculators, not the poor farmer hoping to find and improve cheap land. In addition, states were using land-sale revenue not to systematically drain swamps or build levees, but instead to finance roads, build bridges and public buildings, fund state universities, and line the pockets of railroad companies.

Wisconsin was among fifteen states that eventually benefited from the Swamp Lands Act—which resulted in a national total of nearly 64 million acres. On December 13, 1856, President Franklin Pierce granted to Wisconsin "all such lands remaining unsold" at the time of the passage of the Swamp Lands Act. Among the 2,284 acres total in the state that initially fell under the Swamp Land Act definition, 80 acres were listed in Sections 13 and 14. Troy Marsh, the largest in the Honey Creek Valley area, was earmarked, according to an early county history, to be drained and transformed into dairy land.

In spite of these grand proclamations, no organized statewide reclamation project was put into effect. How could it? The money was being used to fund the state university, build roads, and, according to the 1855 Green Bay Advocate, "to pay off indebtedness for institutions Lunatic and others."

Lucky for Section 13.

### August Night Greeting

At sunset cranes shout loudly in pairs as they return from my neighbor's soybean field. This time of day the smells shift to slurry blackness. Dampness from the marsh takes on a coolness as I approach the edge. I can almost feel the changing of the guard. Swallows and black birds dive and cavort. Frogs ping and boom. *Krack-cher-ACK.* Cranes stare out from shadows of reeds, ghostlike.

I decide to float out with the kayak to inspect the beaver dam. I make my way half-way across the water when a dark thick head swims toward me as big as a dog. Then SLAP Splash! The beaver dives under water and vanishes. I paddle closer to the den, even though I know this is the last place the beaver might appear. The ramshackle pile of chewed branches looks as deserted as a house in a ghost town. I begin to understand the patience of hunters. How necessary it is to wait and linger for just the right moment. Waiting is difficult, but what I'm really doing is leaving myself open for surprise. What I want to appear probably won't. What will appear, however, may be even more amazing.

As I return across the marsh in eerie semi-darkness dragging the kayak over muddy tussocks and boot-sucking traps, I am startled by a strange call. SQUAAAAAAWK! Something the size of a cat prowls up the hill, stopping every so often to peck at the ground. I watch, fascinated. SQUAAAAWWWWK! The immature great horned owl is using its pathetic baby-begging voice as it hunts down a dinner of insects in the dirt. Somewhere high above in a pine tree, its mother observes.

The immature owl makes an ungainly take-off and flies with enormous wings into a branch when it senses my presence. SQUAAAAAWKKK! The bird is learning to hunt its own dinner and complains fiercely to its beleaguered mother. Its cries seem to say, "Mom! I'm hungry! Feed me!" But like a good mother, she keeps her

Fragrant water lilies crowd the stream.

ground and doesn't budge. The immature owl has to learn this important lesson, or it will never survive on its own.

The immature owl makes another swoop back to the ground and hops along in a dejected manner, pecking at the ground for stray locusts and grasshoppers. I wonder if the owl will ever learn how to sing its call the way it's supposed to: WHO COOKS FOR YOU? WHO COOKS FOR YOU ALL? I wonder if it will ever learn to hunt and live up to the fierceness of its nickname, Flying Tiger. A matchless night predator of incredible skill, the great horned owl is feared by nearly every bird.

Fireflies wink and blink. The moon is full and yellow. Frogs ping. A few muffled birds cry.

In the late days of summer the water in the lake takes on a dull scum, unmoving, unmoved—even by wind. I spot floating white swan feathers and dead or struggling insects.

This is a thirsty, waiting time. There has been no rain in a week and the lake water level seems to be shrinking. From the kayak it's possible to see where the higher water line was, dark and green, six inches higher than where it is now.

As the lilies die back, they remind me of crushed debris found under baseball bleachers after a game. White fragrant blossoms shriveled like old paper cups, fist-size leaves dried like wrappers. A few yellow spatterdock remain where the beavers have not yet found them.

Only crickets' incessant chirping rattles the silence as sunset approaches. Soon even their songs will be gone. This is the long slide into the beginning of silence. The marsh begins to smell of decay. I betray my human desire for non-ambiguity. I don't want the seasons to change. Not yet.

# Autumn

"Suddenly out of the north came the
sound I had been waiting for, a soft
melodious gabbling that swelled and
died and increased in volume until all
other sounds were engulfed by its clamor.
Far in the blue I saw them, a long skein
of dots undulating like a floating ribbon
pulled toward the south by an invisible
cord tied to the point of its V."

Sigurd F. Olson,
*The Singing Wilderness*

# *September*

This is where the journey begins. A cool shift in the wind fingers the sedges, back-hands through cattails, and then tosses left and right a bobbing stand of bright goldenrod. A sudden ghost cloud of red-wings, strangely silent, rises up from a hidden place among the bulrush. The birds hover, dart, disappear as if one creature.

Autumn is a time of motion and ambivalence, restlessness and uncertainty that prompts mysterious migrations great and small and rearrangement of families. For me, autumn stands like a wedge between lush, bright plenty and dark, cold want.

Morning sun rises later; evening sun sets earlier. In this growing compression of light, neither I nor the other plants and animals of the marsh ever seem to have enough time to adapt, to prepare for, or flee what we know is coming: the icy grip of winter.

This early September morning haze rides the lake. I set off through the marsh for the canoe. Dew drenches my pant legs. Spiderwebs drape across the muddy path. In dim light the sedges take on the first hints of yellow. The almost imperceptible burnished color reveals that the die-back has begun.

Bonfire smoke lingers beyond the meadow where my neighbor heaped branches and crippled chairs, fence posts and broken cartons and set them afire. This morning what remains is the incense of burning leaves and the odor of must—the smell of the marsh in transition. I take a deep breath and inhale the whiff of damp mud and soggy feather, fallen stalk, and crumpled leaf.

Something is about to happen. Something is about to shift. Even the field crickets can tell. Their chirping is less exuberant, less noisy.

I overturn the canoe and a small, furry brown body scrambles away in terror. My heart leaps. I try to reassure myself that what I saw was only a hiding mouse or small muskrat seeking shelter from the night's cold. Gingerly, I thump the canoe to make sure all stowaways have abandoned ship. Then I haul the canoe to the stream's edge. Sleepy frogs leap. I step inside the canoe and push out into the shallow water.

Paddling is easier now that the beds of lilies have shrunk. The flat lily leaves—once as big as dinner plates—have become brittle and curled. A tangle of overturned leaves—some brown, some frayed—floats on the surface. My paddle crunches through the lily remains. Such effortless movement wasn't possible earlier in the season, when the muscular stems, leaves, and flowers formed a thick barrier throughout the stream.

The few blossoms left uneaten by beavers have collapsed and sunk into the water. Lily stems clipped by beavers thrust upward out of the water like shriveled, accusing fingers. The lily bed, which may be hundreds of years old, expands beneath the stream- and lake-bed mud every growing season with a network of creeping underground stems, rhizomes.

The circular lily leaves, each filled with a network of air spaces, are well-adapted to their waterborne life. The buoyant, leathery leaves with smooth margins help resist tearing by wind and waves. Their flat surfaces provide a perfect platform for dragonfly and damsel-fly take-offs and landings. The broad leaves conceal small fish from predators and hide swimming turtles.

A beetle of the *Donacia* genus finds lily leaves so convenient that the female nibbles holes in the leaf, sticks the lower part of its body into the hole and deposits eggs on the underside of the leaf. When the larvae hatch, they feed on underwater portions of the lily and suck air from the stem like deep-sea scuba divers. When they spin cocoons, they attach their water-tight cases filled with air drawn from the water lily.

The sweet fragrance of white water lilies is so subtle, I can barely detect it. All through summer the teacup shaped white flower with its yellow stamen opens and closes, depending on the light. Now that fall has come, the stream seems strangely empty without the summer blossoms. With the advent of cooler weather, the lilies dip below the water, where the seeds mature inside the fleshy fruit.

In medieval England the water lily's power was believed so remarkable that people picked the flowers at the height of a full moon to use in love potions or to dry and wear as a love amulet. Of course, lily-gatherers had to take certain precautions; they wore ear plugs to avoid being bewitched by the voices of water nymphs that haunted marshy streams and lured unsuspecting folks to watery deaths.

Even if I wanted to make an amulet, I'm too late. The water lily prime is past. I can not find one blossom remaining.

As I move into the open water of the lake I notice that the skimmings of bugs and algae that drifted yesterday on the surface are gone. I stick my finger into the cool, limpid water and spy darting fish. As the air temperature drops each night, the surface temperature of the lake has begun to drop as well. The cooler surface layer of water becomes denser, heavier, and sinks, carrying along with it dissolved oxygen and nutrients and plant material. Eventually, warmer water from deep in the lake and stream is pushed up to the surface.

This dance between the upper and lower layers of the water is called the "fall overturn," an ugly name for a subtle but essential shift. The water temperature change occurs slowly, ensuring that plants, animals, and fish that live beneath the water can adapt in time before the water reaches 39 degrees Fahrenheit. Eventually, as the surface temperature drops further, ice forms and floats.

Without the seasonal cycling of surface and deep water, the bottom of the stream and lake would soon be starved of oxygen. Eventually, the nutrients would remain at the bottom and the lake and stream would die.

Between dense stands of cattails on shore and a few yellowing bunches of common arrowhead, I spot assorted abandoned redwing nests, lost feathers, a painted turtle's shell, the curved, white twisted home of a snail or scud, the crayfish tail from a raccoon's dinner. The helter-skelter stand of cattails includes this year's and past years' growth all tangled together.

Looking deeply into the accumulated live and dead remnants of one year in the marsh is like examining the crowded attic of a reclusive pack rat. Nature is prolific and wasteful, a churning factory of biomass. And yet I can only look on the such fecundity in wonder. There's something profoundly optimistic about this towering stack of chaotic stem and seed and leaf. Something, I tell myself, must be worth living for and dying for if the same process happens again and again, season after season, year after year.

Unlike a walk in the woods in fall, there's no bright, dramatic signal of the change in seasons in the marsh. There's no wild, splashy change in leaf color, no moment leaves drop. There are few obvious nuts or easily identifiable fruits, such as acorns or ripe wild apples. What happens in the marsh as plants prepare for winter is subtle. It requires investigating at all levels—above, on, and below the water's surface.

As I drift in the canoe, I can see below me an entire forest of plants: ribbonlike strands of wild celery, broad-arching leaves of pondweed, bottle-brush stems of coon tail, and the waving feathery branches of milfoil. Underwater plants have poetic names like quillwort, clasping-leaf pondweed, and slender naiad, which dances like their namesake mythical water nymphs, gentle water creatures capable of cruel revenge. Each of these have adapted with a number of strategies for reproductive survival.

Triggered by changes in light and temperature, the feathery milfoil at this very moment is producing winter buds, shortened branches with tightly spaced, often reduced leaves. They may look no different from severed pieces of plants as they float to the lake bed, but each section of a bud contains within it all that's required to create another milfoil next spring.

Ducks gabble noisily around the bend as I approach the inlet to the spring. The mallards and coots have been busily gulping drifting clumps of duckweed, an free-floating green plant that is individually only the size of piece of confetti. Each duckweed has a tiny dangling root and such a minuscule flower you need a magnifying glass to see it when it blooms in late summer. In autumn the tiny duck weed is getting ready to survive. These small plants also produce new winter buds that lose buoyancy and sink to the bottom to wait for spring and begin growing.

I paddle and pause. Something snaps and crackles nearby. A diving turtle along the water's edge has set off hundreds of smacking carnivorous traps in the tangled mat of creeping bladderwort. Who would suspect that a plant with a delicate, yellow snapdragon-like flower hovering above the water's surface could be so bloodthirsty? Tiny air-filled, bladder-like traps, clinging to submerged stems capture small prey ranging in size from one-celled protozoan creatures to mosquito larvae.

Each bladderwort trap is ingeniously designed with an entrance, a flaplike hinged door made watertight by a layer of mucilage. Antennae-like projections and trigger hairs help guide unsuspecting prey toward the trap door that's covered with an attractive sugary mucilage. Only a slight brush against the trigger hairs and the prey is swept inside by a rush of water. With the efficiency of science fiction film monsters, the traps slam shut in less than 1/500 of a second. Trapped prey dies and is digested by plant enzymes.

In fall the creeping bladderwort prepares to survive the winter by what appears to be disintegration. What's really happening is that bladderwort stem fragments break away and float to the bottom to rest in the sediment. As soon as the water begins to warm in spring, the stems will grow new plants.

Wild celery, or eelgrass, is considered among the premier source of food for migrating waterfowl in fall. All parts of this plant are eagerly eaten, from rhizomes to tubers (roots) and fruit. Wild celery leaves have a consistency of cellophane. Nothing surpasses the romantic cleverness of the reproductive capabilities of this plant. What other submerged wetland plant sends love letters to itself?

A few months earlier, in midsummer, wild celery floats to the surface male flowers that are actually closed floral envelopes. Each envelope contains an air bubble that lifts it to the surface, where it opens and creates a kind of sail that allows the male flower to shimmer and wend its way across the surface. Meanwhile, tiny white female flowers, which developed under water, rise to the surface on fast-growing spiral coiled stalks. These flowers bob along the surface, creating dips in the surface tension so that when one of the male flowers in full sail happens by, it will glide into and pollinate the female flower.

Once fertilized after this complex ritual, the female flower retracts beneath the surface and develops into a podlike fruit—a capsular treat of special tastiness to visiting waterfowl who eat, digest, and defecate the seeds—spreading the eelgrass further—on migratory journeys to other lakes and ponds.

When I finally reach the beaver lodge, I discover no one is home, no one except a two-foot long Northern water snake curled comfortably on the beavers' sunny roof. The brown snake patterned with reddish-brown and black saddle shapes is a handsome one—though it's among the most persecuted. People kill water snakes out of fear or ignorance, believing that it preys on game fish.

The harmless snake does not move, but I know it must have sensed the trembling when bow of the canoe bumped the beaver lodge. It flicks its tongue to pick up chemicals from the ground and air and brings them into its mouth. This combined sense of taste and smell helps the snake detect food—or enemies. When hunting frisky frogs, tadpoles, and crayfish, the Northern water snake makes ample use of its eyesight and sense of smell.

Something about me must smell and taste dangerous. Slowly, the snake lowers itself from chewed branch to limb along the lodge roof. I catch a glimpse of its distinctive white underside decorated with bright red half-moons. Then, in a flash, the snake plunges into the lake, throwing its body into a series of curves, pushing against the water surface with the back of each curve. I watch, hypnotized, as the snake undulates across the water. The swimming snake seems to defy gravity. Why doesn't it drown? Why doesn't it sink? How is it that bending and unbending propels it so neatly atop the water? I think of the ancient effigy mound, whose long, narrow shape mimics the water snake.

In a month—maybe less—the water snake's swimming will end. It will find a few fellow snakes and curl up in an overbank root system or perhaps a hidden crevice of my basement wall to hibernate until April.

In late September on a clear day following a thunderstorm, while standing in the marsh one afternoon I hear a faint noise. I look up and can see nothing. A plaintive call goes out between the pair of sandhill cranes that made a small tussocky island in the stream their nesting home. Overhead the sound echoes like a faraway shout inside an old-fashioned cistern or the cacophony of a music box tumbling down a flight of stairs. Slowly, the sound grows louder. The flock of cranes heading south looks like a slender skein of string tangling and untangling. The cranes ride south buoyed on thermals, energy-saving air currents created by rising air temperature, I shield my eyes and squint skyward. Where are they going? How do they know how to get there?

"Farewell!" the cranes seem to shout. Their cries sound alternately amused and outraged. They won't be back again until late February or early March.

As a child on long family road trips, I had the egocentric notion that after our crowded station wagon passed through a small town somewhere in Nebraska or Iowa or Kansas, that town simply disappeared; the main street, grain elevator, and railroad crossing simply ceased to exist.

And yet now I am the one left behind. I am the witness standing far, far below on the ground watching the multitude of birds departing, birds passing through. For the next month or more, the sky will be filled with Canada geese from Hudson's Bay heading farther south, black coots en route to Central America, and red-winged blackbirds bound for Mexico.

As the first great flock of sandhills passes overhead on their way to Florida, I wonder if can they see me? Or do I, too, simply disappear from their minds—a harmless, puny human waving at them from the edge of the marsh?

The restlessness and the swooping sound day and night of birds calling, wheeling, streaming across the sky mesmerizes me. On the night of a full moon geese squabble. The next afternoon, a clear one in which the aspen around the wetland have turned golden, buteos, accipiters, ospreys, and falcons pass overhead. They're riding what naturalist Frances Hamerstrom called, "the winds of the great travel lanes."

What seem like mixed flocks of red-tailed hawks and Cooper's hawks are only smaller flocks sharing the same currents. Of all the hawks that travel through Wisconsin, according to Hamerstrom, only the broad-winged travel in great flocks, called "kettles."

Above the wetland, a harrier, also called a marsh hawk, soars then skims over the tops of sedges in search of mice. I haven't seen this raptor with its distinctive white rump patch and black-tipped wings since last fall, when it only stopped by, perhaps on its way to Central America. The other autumnal marsh visitor heading the same direction is the broad-winged hawk, the smallest buteo in Wisconsin. This small hawk perches in the trees near the edge of the wetland to harass young crows. The broad-winged appears to enjoy nothing more than fresh frog, which it daintily skins before eating. Frog skin, according to hawks, has a nasty flavor.

There are those of us who stay. We have no choice but to adjust and find a way to remain beside the wetland all winter. Some wetland residents begin to adapt by storing food everywhere. This is the compulsive activity of black-capped chickadees that dart out into the wetland for thistle seeds then zip back to the edge to hide their treasures in the bark of trees. Already this fall beavers managed to topple half a dozen aspen from my neighbor's property, then drag them to their newest lodge to store woody stems and tender bark for snacks later in winter.

Muskrats have already begun preparing for winter by building houses made of cattail and bulrush. These dens are sloppy affairs, constructed like miniature haystacks three to four feet in diameter and up to three to four feet in height from the surface of the water, with underwater entrances.

A muskrat house is hastily built and often smells sharply of rich, sweet, yellow musk—the namesake glandular odor produced by muskrats. After one season a lodge is often abandoned. That's when other wetland residents, such as mice, raccoons, and minks move in. Terns and ducks build nests atop the roof. Mites and insects crawl among the walls. Scuds, or snails, cling below the water level and nibble the foundation as it rots. Minnows and bullheads have been known to find food and shelter in underwater lodge passageways.

Unlike beavers, muskrats do not store food for the winter. In autumn the brown, three-pound adult males, which look like oversized meadow mice, gorge themselves so completely, they seem barely to waddle about on land. From a distance, the swimming muskrat, sculling along with its hind feet, produces a distinctive V-shaped wake. I watch for muskrats in the water but find none this morning. Supposedly it's possible to call a muskrat with a whistle made with thin strips of birch bark held within a split twig; its sound imitates the muskrat's squeak. No one I know has been able to copy, however, the muskrat's angry teeth chatter or hiss.

Everywhere I paddle along the edge of the lake I see signs of muskrat nibblings: floating gnawed sedge stems and lily roots. When there's plenty of food, as there is now, muskrats are picky but wasteful eaters. Never careful planners, muskrats will eat their houses if food becomes scarce in winter. They have been known to eat their own tails, their children, and their mates when winter starvation hits.

## October

While so much adaptation and preparation and migration is going on, there is another aspect to the restlessness, which has to do with family dynamics. In the wetland there are countless adult animals forcing their children out into the world. Every night for the last two weeks I have heard coyotes' plaintive yipping and howling in the night. In the fall the social organization of the pack undergoes shuffling as some of the spring season's pups are forced out on their own. Availability of unclaimed territory and food all play a part in the shifting dynamic of the pack.

Out on the lake the mute swan family seems to be undergoing obvious strains as the parents attempt to force off the lake the three surviving grown cygnets. Mute swans are neither native or migratory. They were introduced to this part of Wisconsin from England in the 1950s. Fiercely loyal to their mates, mute swans intimidate territory invaders by impressive busking, cruising while holding their wings in puffed up attack mode. If all else fails in dissuading another swan intruder, they flap their seven-foot wing span with great energy, take off, and dive-bomb one another. The wings of a thirty-pound male swan in flight thrum against the air with an eerie, metallic sound.

I wake to the sound of laughing geese, which seem to taunt, "Still asleep, fool? You missed your chance." There are many similarities between goose hunters and photographers. We both wear bright orange. We wake early. We seldom see what we hope to find.

Foolishly, I paddle out into the stream—in spite of a warning by the swans who take off with a great noisy *whump whump whump.* Goose hunting, I have been told, begins tomorrow. I have one day left to capture the arriving and departing multitudes of Canadas. At the mouth of the stream, I spy a large group of geese placidly engaged in what geese do best: eating and floating. As I grow closer, I begin to think that these are the stupidest geese I have ever encountered. Why do they remain so still, so tame?

Suddenly, a horrible squawk fills the air. The unmistakable sound of a human making a goose call. I freeze. A hunter in a camouflage cap pokes his head up from the duck blind and shouts, "How long you been there?"

"A few minutes," I lie. I can barely speak, I'm so terrified. The hunter looks equally disturbed. He sees my camera. He knows he's breaking the law by shooting before the season officially begins. "Goose?" I ask.

The hunter nods impatiently.

"On the lake?"

He nods again.

"I'm going back upriver now," I say in a voice as nonchalant as I can muster. Nervously, I pray he'll keep looking out on the lake, where the geese will not land again until after sundown, when all shooting ceases.

I quickly turn the kayak and head in the opposite direction. Although no shots are fired the rest of the day, I feel no relief. For me the hunting season is always an oppressive time of year. For several months, I cannot safely meander the marsh. How odd to think that the wetland is most dangerous not because of any wild animal, but because of other humans.

### Killing Frost

The exhalation of swamps is a peculiar odor, a kind of earthy attic smell or the odor of an old drawer suddenly opened after being closed for a very long time. It is the scent of memory, of unknown language. At sunset in October, as I walk back through the marsh toward the copse of aspen, the smell wafts everywhere around me, sunlight released, the coolness of night already descending. A kind of trading of places.

I was mystified about why this exhalation occurs until I read a booklet published in 1920 by the U.S. Department of Agriculture

Bureau of Soils that says, "Loose spongy soil of peat marshes does not conduct the heat received from the sun during the day downward." Lower layers of soil don't become warmed in peat marshes as they do in more earthy soils. As soon as the sun begins to set, the wetland exhales daylight warmth like the generous sigh of a sleeping man.

As autumn arrives, the first killing frost glitters in early morning on the marsh—and nowhere else. Uplands and hillsides remain frost-free, but the marsh has speeded the season forward by two weeks or more. Again the 1920 soil survey attempts to explain these strange climatic variations. "Cold air which forms on the surface of all the ground at night," the booklet says, "tends to flow down and collect in low places."

The early fall frost in the marsh lurks and kills corn, which obviously provides yet another reason not to drain the wetland and plant crops. The soil survey, refusing to admit the obvious, provides more perky, desperate advice for farmers: "This difficulty with peat marshes can be overcome, to a certain extent by heavy rolling, which, by compacting the soil, permits the heat to be conducted downward more readily."

## Of Ditches and Dreams

On April 13, 1910, the owners of land that happened to overlap the Honey Creek Marsh filed with the circuit court clerk to create their own commission for digging a grand drainage ditch. Two years later, work began. Ditch-diggers created a 5.375 mile–long ditch, two to twelve feet deep, engineered as a kind of funneling system, with an eighteen-foot fall, or descent in elevation, to drain marsh water into smaller connecting ditches.

By 1936 the ditch had thoroughly done its job: Troy Marsh had vanished. The water was sucked away by ditches, and the land was plowed. Without plentiful sedges and cattails, waterfowl disappeared. Frogs leapt into the ditches to make their escape.

What had once been the biggest wetland in the township intersected by winding, disorderly Honey Creek is now gone completely. Hardly a trace of its existence remains. The wetland and crooked creek have been replaced by level fields covered with row upon row of mechanically planted, evenly spaced feed corn, replaced in alternate

Swallowtail visits a wetland thistle on its migration.

years with soybeans. A network of ruler-straight, sterile ditches feeds the larger ditch. Gone are the cattails and sedges that once grew in chaotic profusion. Gone are the geese, the red-winged blackbirds, the marsh wrens.

It takes a great deal of imagination to picture a wild creek with fish and freshwater mussels tumbling through here. Along the banks were aquatic plants like arrowhead and lotus and, according to local legend, a small group of hollow oaks filled with a honey-bee hive that once gave the creek its name.

The results of the Troy Drainage Ditch are stark. In 1936 the Wisconsin Land Economic Survey was authorized by state law to "promote more complete and practical utilization of land in Wisconsin." Field workers, mostly trained forestry graduates from Wisconsin universities, crossed the land at intervals of one-half mile and mapped in detail vegetation, soil types, topography particulars, roads, and houses of the entire state. The field workers counted exactly how many acres of marsh were left in the four sections affected by the Troy Drainage Ditch. At that time, only a total of 129 acres of grass and sedge marsh survived. This is remarkable, considering that in

1836, exactly 100 years earlier, the surveyors who first came here tallied a total of more than 1500 acres of grass and sedge marsh in the same four sections. The wetland loss, thanks to the drainage ditch, was nearly 86 percent.

Did anyone beside muskrats mourn Troy Marsh's passing?

The Troy Drainage Ditch was dug only a little more than a mile from the wetland where I live. The very closeness and the thoroughness of its efficiency are chilling examples of how easily and irrevocably a wetland can be obliterated. What's even more disturbing is the realization that what happened to Troy Marsh could easily have happened here.

The 1936 Wisconsin Land Economic Survey of the 640 acres in Section 13 showed that only 77 acres in the section had been cleared—compared with 398 in the neighboring Section 14 or 547 in Section 12. Section 13 had 83 acres of "permanent pasture." Marsh land accounted for 75 acres of cattails, 10 of marsh grass, 125 of sedge grass, and 124 acres of water. While total marsh land in the county was about 18.7 percent, total marsh land in Section 13 was a surprisingly healthy 46 percent.

Why the high marsh survival rate in Section 13—and not elsewhere? Perhaps it had to do with lack of capital and landowner motivation. The three well-heeled farmers who backed the Troy Drainage Ditch had extensive acreage and were willing to work together. Necessary financial backing and cooperation for a drainage project may not have existed among the land owners in Section 13.

After the Troy Drainage Ditch was completed, a 1920s drainage boom throughout southeastern and elsewhere in Wisconsin created extensive schemes, many of which were promoted by active drainage propaganda in farming journals and newspapers. But the process was still expensive. It involved first surveying the land carefully, figuring out where to dig the trenches, then carefully laying with exact measurements factory-produced cylindrical drainage tiles with precise leveling at a depth of four feet or more. One foot or more in length and with diameters of two to eight inches, the drainage tiles, which were often made of concrete, looked a little like sewer pipes. After they were lowered into the ditch and connected together, they were covered with dirt. Unlike open drainage ditches, farmers did not have to clean out fallen trees or other debris that blocked flow.

The cost of installing drainage tiles, however, remained high. It was "justified only on land whose potential value was exceptionally high," historian Hugh Prince wrote in *Wetlands of the American Midwest.*

Fortunately for the wetland in Section 13, the land did not have "exceptionally high" agricultural potential. Too much of it was sandy and rocky. According to the 1924 U.S. Geological Survey Soil Map, the wetland soil was deemed "low-lying peat."

"Natural drainage is extremely poor," the Bureau of Soils report warned. "Some of it is subject to overflow and over a great deal of it the water table remains close to the surface most of the time." The report described this part of Walworth County very explicitly. "Treeless in part and . . . covered with a growth of sphagnum moss and coarse marsh grasses."

> Many outlet ditches have been or are being constructed, but in most cases only the outlet ditches have been constructed and lateral open ditches or tile drains have not yet been put in. When this land is thoroughly drained and properly fertilized, it will be adapted to a number of crops, including corn, sugar beets, cabbage, onions, and hay. . . . Until thorough drainage is supplied it is useless to attempt cultivation. At present the Peat marshes are used chiefly for production of marsh hay and some pasture. . . . Little tiling has been done on the Peat lands, but the importance of this is being appreciated and more attention than ever before is being given to the reclamation of the marsh lands.

"Make every acre on each farm productive," was the battle cry of the 1920s. Promises were made by the governmental agriculture officials that drained marshes could become as valuable and productive as any other land in the county. These claims, however, soon proved to be only wishful thinking.

From 1910 to 1914, around the same time the Troy Drainage Ditch was created, another ditch was dug two hundred miles to the north, in the Horicon Swamp, a 32,000-acre area of wetland and open water. Once drained, Horicon peat had properties no one fully predicted. When exposed to air, it quickly oxidized into muck. As soon as the muck turned powder dry, wind easily eroded it. Only a few years later, after crops suffered from steadily declining fertility and an "undesirable taste," a fire broke out, after which the drained wetland burned underground for nearly twelve years.

Not until 1921 did a group of local conservation-minded citizens band together to try to restore the wetland by reopening the ditches and reflooding the badly scarred acreage. In 1927 the Wisconsin Legislature passed the Horicon Marsh Wildlife Refuge Bill to restore marshland water levels and acquire more land. Today the Horicon marsh is one of the largest freshwater marshes in the United States—a happy ending to an otherwise devastating wetland drainage story.

Clearly, whatever fertility reclaimed or drained wetlands had in the first years swiftly declined with time. "High water-retaining capacity of original peat and its consequent ability to store water and temper flow of streams would have been of greater value to the entire economy of the state," writes John T. Curtis in his exhaustive *Vegetation of Wisconsin,* "than any temporary returns gained by a few owners at the price of destruction of the (wetland) reservoirs."

On a clear, late October night my husband and I enter the marsh. All day it rained, but tonight the moon rises full and hangs over the horizon large and yellow and grinning. The marsh fills with shadows. We walk out along the muddy path. There's no need for flashlights. Even the puddles reflect moonlight. So do the stems of quivering bulrush and leaves of cattail. The place is alive with shadow, with sound.

Something splutters and rustles—perhaps along the flooded muskrat trail. Footsteps plod. Water churns. Something munches away. Who is it? What is it? Unable to see the animal, my imagination creates an enormous, toothy gray wolf, even though I know it is probably nothing more than a clumsy, hungry raccoon. Gradually the noise vanishes. More splashing. The crazy laughter of a duck.

A flock of Canadas, newly arrived in the lake, raucously reprimand each other. When they came in for a landing earlier at sundown, they roared as loudly as semi trucks passing on the freeway.

The geese whiffled, tumbled, almost spun as they extended their webbed feet for a noisy landing on to the lake.

Now they sound as if they are saying: "You're blocking my view!" and "You brought the wrong video." Then two geese, perhaps the unsociable ones who ruined the evening for everyone, fly off in silence. So close are their beating wings, I can feel the air riffle against my cheeks as they pass.

## November

Strange nightmare. I'm exploring the swamp and from under a board or from behind the house where the trees have fallen over at the edge of the wetland emerge three or four men with pumpkin heads. Almost like mushrooms. Half animal, half plant, they bob up and down, waving their arms as if they're brainless scarecrows in *The Wizard of Oz*. Who are they? What are they doing there? I can't really tell.

Yellow is the color of November, the month my father died. Every November yellow smothers the aspen leaves at the edge of the wetland with a brilliance that aches in my eyes. Every November my father dies again. *Hurry, drop leaves. Be done with it.* Don't linger, I want to say. Make death swift.

Little by little, I've come to realize there's no avoiding the yellow of November. There's no avoiding death. Yellow was always present—even in June, a month filled with new life.

The marsh taught me this.

What I've always perceived as green in new tender leaves, stems, and stalks in spring is colored by a pigment called chlorophyll—necessary to the leaf's food production. In the beginning, abundant chlorophyll simply masked yellow, which is created by compounds with impossible names: carotenoids and xanthophylls. They're the same pigments that make egg yolks, cream, and butter yellow. Yellow was there in the leaves in spring. Yellow was there in the leaves in summer. But I couldn't see it yet.

Only in the fall when a tree senses shortening days does its relationship with its leaves shift. There's a kind of pull-back of resources—especially water and nutrients—until finally the leaves are altogether abandoned. When I pick up a fallen aspen leaf, it is part yellow, part green. The chlorophyll is beginning to break down; as it disappears, the underlying yellow is gradually revealed, until the entire aspen is shingled in a kind of golden glow.

I cannot escape death. Neither can the aspen leaves. Out in the wetland the yellow sedges bend and billow like waves. These leaves and stems, too, will eventually fall to the ground. Even then their contribution has not ended. Although the leaves are dead, they are still filled with organic compounds and minerals. Insects, worms, snails, and other creatures will consume these parts of the leaf so that they can live. Chemicals from deep in the muck and peat will mingle with standing marsh water and break down the leaf even further, until it transforms into the rich dark muck that helps support all wetland life. This transformation is never-ending.

In the same way vegetation lives on in other forms to benefit other creatures and plants, so too, I've come to realize, my father lives on in me, my children, my brothers and sisters—in all the lives he touched.

On the last kayaking trip of the season, the afternoon is bitter and gray. I venture out into the stream and discover a thin film of ice on the lake at the edges. As the kayak cuts through, it sounds like shattering glass. Few birds of any kind fly past. No turtles. No frogs. No floating vegetation. It's as if the lake has been wiped clean.

Crushing cold wind blows. Because I forgot my gloves, I have to keep my sleeves down around my hands and paddle without my thumbs. It is a tricky operation, one that makes me appreciate the challenges of being a thumbless fox or snake. Of course, I've never seen a fox or snake kayaking on the lake in mid-November before. Perhaps they're far too sensible.

When I return to the boat landing and pull the kayak to the path, the frozen ground crunches beneath my feet and gives way at unexpected moments. A lone harrier circles overhead. He dips up and down as if to flash a white gleaming greeting. And at that moment, something fine as feathers floats from the sky. First snow.

### A Visit from Ghosts

On June 22, 1936, a university-trained forestry employee named Charles Neubert visited the wetland and scribbled his own observations.

Neubert had been hired by the state of Wisconsin as part of a small army of field workers with the Land Economic Survey who were supposed to cross the land at intervals of one-half mile to describe topography, analyze soil, measure trees, and tally wild life in every section in every county in the state. His job was to detail everything he noticed—from types of crops, roads, and houses to locations of cemeteries, cheese factories, and bathing beaches.

Times were hard. Wisconsin and the rest of the country were still reeling from massive unemployment, business bankruptcy, crop failures, and farm foreclosures of the Great Depression. The idea behind the survey's massive, hopeful effort was to systematically amass facts about Wisconsin's landscape and then come up with a plan to use resources that had not already been squandered.

Clearly, mistakes had been made. Farming during World War I had overexpanded. Land was plowed that should have been left as range or pasture. After several consecutive years of drought in parts of Wisconsin and elsewhere in the Midwest, wind had eroded what was left of good topsoil. Farms were abandoned. Wasteful lumbering operations in the northern part of Wisconsin created abandoned cutover acreage. Unwisely planned wetland drainage projects caused further wasted or "unsuitable" lands. The goal stated by the Wisconsin Land Economic Survey was to "promote a more complete and practical utilization of the land." The first step was to categorize what was available.

When Neubert set out on that summer solstice day, the landscape in Section 13 must have been fairly empty of people. On his two-mile walk north along an unimproved gravel road, he marked only three small squares to indicate houses. Two were "seasonal," which meant they were only occupied in summer. Stretching to the east was sedge marsh and to the west pasture. He passed cattail marsh, crossed the stream that flowed under the road through a culvert, and paused to

Below the bur oak (left) flows a pure spring.

note a small stand of popple with some birch. He climbed a small hill used for pasturing cows and was able to spy in the distance the lake. On his map he marked a spring beneath a big oak at the inlet, yet the only wildlife he recorded was one Hungarian partridge.

Neubert's hieroglyphics scrawled on the inventory map provide a maddeningly incomplete picture of Section 13. What I want to know is what the wetland sounded and smelled like in the early part of the twentieth century. What was blooming? What was darting overhead or scuttling along the ground?

As I struggle with Neubert's crude map to recreate in my own mind the landscape in the 1920s and 1930s, something remarkable happens. I am visited by ghosts.

One morning as I sit at my desk, two strangers knock at the door—almost as if summoned by my imagination. I glance out the window at a couple getting out of a Buick with Illinois license plates. Automatically, I assume the couple are Jehovah's Witnesses.

I'm wrong. They haven't come to convert me. They've come, I soon discover, to try to recapture the experience of a landscape they'd cherished but not seen for more than sixty years.

"My father used to own this land," the man explains hurriedly as I try and restrain my large, lunging dogs. "We spent summers here in a cottage on seventy acres back in the thirties. We just wanted to—"

"See it again," the woman finishes his sentence for him. He seems grateful. They introduce themselves as Bill Baum and Barbara Vitkovits.

Bill, tan and dressed nattily in white pants, floral shirt, shiny shoes, has a pleasant, engaging smile. Balding and trim, he has the compact, steady movements of a golfer in his early sixties. Barbara is an attractive woman who looks no more than sixty. She fingers the pale chiffon scarf knotted around her neck. Her nails are painted deep red. She stands in patent leather sandals a safe distance from the door. Clearly, the large, howling dogs make her nervous.

Flabbergasted by my good fortune, I agree to show them around. I rush back inside the house to grab a notepad and change into different shoes. For the first time I stop to consider how I must look to them in my usual awful writer's garb: gray sweatpants, a too-big T-shirt decorated with sea turtles, green house slippers.

As we wander around the front yard, their remarkable love story unfolds. All through grade school, Barbara says, she and Bill knew each other. They were high school sweethearts even though her parents forbade her to see him.

I sneak a glance at Bill, who calmly wipes his glasses with a tissue. It's hard to imagine him as a wild young buck.

This place was where they met secretly, she says. There's something wistful about the way she glances down the hill and out beyond the wetland. I wonder what she's remembering. To get here she took the bus from Milwaukee, then walked through cornfields. "It was all innocent," she says. Picking wild raspberries. Finding arrowheads. Rowing boats and swimming. He once tried to put a frog in her pants.

A few years later, their lives veered in different directions. They parted. Each married twice. Each divorced. For forty years they did not see each other. And then, by some remarkable chance, they met again. They now live together in California.

"We're back here for a high school reunion," he explains. "We thought it would be a good chance to see the place again."

As we walk around, what appears to amaze them the most are the trees. When Bill first came here as a young boy, the view all the way down to the wetland from the top of the sandy, rocky hill was unobstructed by trees or anything else. "Just some underbrush and a few bur oaks standing by themselves," he says. "A few shrubby willows by the edge of the marsh—that was all." The red pines and elms and apple trees were nothing more than small saplings he and his father planted one summer. Now they tower overhead, some fifty feet or more.

There were two houses on the property in the 1920s when his family initially came here to spend summer weekends. Originally, they stayed at the bottom of the hill in a tin shack that smelled of kerosene from the stove and lamps and stale cigarette smoke from "the people who'd come over the years to play cards," says Bill. At the top of the hill was a larger, wooden cottage with three small bedrooms and a screened porch. Without running water, plumbing, or electricity, this was where Bill, his younger sister and parents stayed on weekends in subsequent years. "I thought it was grand," he says.

In 1944 his parents bought the cottage and the entire seventy-acre property, including part of the wetland and a farmhouse to the south. A few years later, they finally installed electricity and built a cinder-block garage. Bill and his sister always referred to their property as "the farm."

Today most everything he remembered about the farm is gone. The cottage and tin shack were torn down years ago. The hand pump and outhouse have been removed. The boardwalk to the stream has long since disappeared. What have not changed as visibly are the wetland, stream, and lake. Bill sniffs. "It smells the same, too," he says and smiles.

Returning to the wetland seems to be a chance for Bill to go back in time. "I consider my years here the happiest in my life," he says. "I was young, carefree, healthy, and in a sportsmen's paradise."

Fall was his favorite season, when nights were cooler and days were sunny. In the 1930s and 1940s few laws restricted hunting. He enjoyed shooting pheasant that roamed the wetland edge and the fields beyond. The lake teemed with blue-winged teal, canvas backs, mallards, and noisy mudhens.

As a teenager he rented a rowboat from a neighbor and went out on to the lake to catch "a nice mess" of blue gills, sunfish, bull-head, and an occasional muddy-tasting black bass. Before there were fishing limits, he once caught twenty-seven crappies, weighing a total of thirty-two pounds, in one day.

"I grew to love the wetland," he says. For him, it was "a wondrous place teeming with life," including herons, muskrats, frogs, water snakes, and huge snapping turtles. What he can't recall are Canada geese, deer, turkeys, and sandhill cranes—all of which were over-hunted sixty years ago and have since made a remarkable comeback.

When it's time for them to leave, Bill promises to send me some old black and white photographs of the place and put me in contact with his sister. As he opens the car door for Barbara, he seems clearly moved by their visit. "I am so relieved," I hear him tell Barbara before he slides behind the steering wheel. They wave to me and drive away.

I am relieved, too. It is a marvelous discovery to encounter people who love a place as much as I do.

Later, the photographs he sends me reveal a wide-open, almost barren place. The lake glitters in the background. The one familiar— though smaller—oak tree stands on the hill all by itself with beseeching branches spread open wide. In the distance stretches the wetland, which somehow looks so much bigger, vaster. It's the presence of the surviving garage, though, that provides me with a point of reference.

I now understand why Bill was so bewildered when he and Barbara came for a visit. The change is startling. Perhaps Thomas Wolfe's 1940 book title is truer than I like to believe. *You can't go home again.* Home changes. So do we.

When I consider the incredible luck of Section 13 and this wetland, I must also consider Bill and Barbara's fortune, too. What are the odds that they would find each other again after forty years of being separated? And what are the odds that I would be sitting at my desk the afternoon that they decided to revisit the land of their youth and first love? Another remarkable gift that comes my way as a result of this encounter is that Bill puts me in touch with his younger sister, Lee.

I know I have found a kindred spirit when she writes to me of her memories and says, "What I liked and can still remember is the oozy, swampy, kind of primeval smell from the swamp on warm, muggy evenings."

As a young girl, Lee was sometimes accompanied by her best friend, Ginny, on family weekend trips. The two girls wandered around the marsh to secret spots where they picked watercress growing in a cold, clear spring beneath a big oak tree. Sometimes they dug for valuable treasure among the ruins of an old barn and found horse bones.

Lee said when she was about twelve years old, she and her friend would walk out on the boardwalk to the stream. "At the pier we would sometimes take the rowboat out on the lake and smoke cigarettes or just jump in and swim. Ginny didn't know how to swim, but she went in anyway. Sometimes we just lay on the end of the pier and looked down into the incredibly clear water to see the little fishes, weeds, and water bugs."

The wetland had its own colorful human characters as well. An

In the 1930s the fen and marsh—almost completely treeless—stretch in the distance behind a frolicking dog and his youthful owner. Courtesy William Baum.

old man named Bill who lived in a farmhouse down the road was "a rough looking, beer bellied, grizzled old man," Lee said, "who spent most of his time chewing tobacco and leaning back against his small house on a kitchen chair out in the sun." Rumor was that he murdered his skinny, ancient housekeeper by pushing her down the steep stairs from the second floor.

Most of Lee's colorful stories about their wetland neighbors were told to her by her father. He claimed that old Bill made moonshine and hid the bottles under the boardwalk that was laid out through the marsh to the stream that led to the lake. The lake, her father warned her, was "very, very deep."

One time, her father liked to tell, old Bill and his friend named Turk got very drunk and went out in the lake in a boat. "Somehow Turk fell in and drowned," Lee said. "When the authorities could not find the body, Bill said he knew how to do it. He got a quart of moonshine, got in the boat and went out onto the lake, raised the bottle up high and called, 'Come on, Turk, come and have a drink.' Dad said the body rose up in the water."

The next morning I wake up early and watch the mist making

ghostly motions across the surface of the lake. I can't help but think of Turk.

Lee, who now resides in northern Wisconsin with her husband, turns out to have lived the longest beside the wetland of anyone I've met. She spent nearly twenty-six years here—from 1932, the year she was born in Milwaukee, until 1958. When she returned in 2003 for a brief visit to see the farm again after an absence of almost fifty years, she described the shock as "a punch to the belly—it had changed *that* much."

She and her husband strolled about picking up windfall apples from the tree her father had planted so long ago. Later, she wrote to me in a letter of her amazement at the growth of trees near the place where their cottage once stood. "Why did I think nothing would grow there? When we bought our place [their current home in northern Wisconsin] in 1983 we immediately set out to change it, cut down trees and plant others, tear down the old buildings and build new ones, make gardens, make a larger pond."

As she left our property with her husband, she turned to him and said, "We want to change things, but we want the places where we have lived to stay the same."

Change has been profound in the county and the surrounding area due to rapid population growth and construction during the past fifty years. What in the 1930s was a sleepy, dirt road from Milwaukee became a four-lane highway. Even the farm's nearest major gravel road, once traveled only by farmers in wagons "because there was no where to go" has become paved and discovered by truckers looking for a shortcut and motorcyclists seeking thrills. The county today is one of the fastest growing in the state.

In 1920, when Lee and Bill's father first came here to hunt ducks with his friends, the population of Walworth County was 29,327, and more than 70 percent of the residents considered themselves "rural." By 2001 the population skyrocketed to 95,200, and fewer than 45 percent of residents considered themselves to be rural.

Throughout the twentieth century boom in tract housing, shopping centers, and golf courses, several farsighted organizations have proven heroic in preserving, protecting, and promoting awareness of the natural landscape. Established in 1936, the Kettle Moraine State Forest, Southern Unit, now encompasses 21,000 acres of forests, meadows, and wetlands. Since 1961, the Nature Conservancy has been working with local communities and landowners to help plan, restore, and manage natural resources in Wisconsin. During the 1970s and 1980s, land for 120 miles of trails in southeastern Wisconsin was developed into a national scenic trail by the Ice Age Park and Trail Foundation.

In 1985 the Nature Conservancy became interested and involved in the Mukwonago River and its watershed of interconnecting streams and numerous wetlands in southeastern Wisconsin. What makes this place unusual is the clear quality of the eighteen-mile Mukwonago, which has helped deem this the "most biodiverse river in southern Wisconsin." The only other rivers that match the quality and variety of species present are the Mississippi and the Wisconsin Rivers, which are much larger.

The river and its wetlands are so remarkable that they have been named by the Nature Conservancy as one of three international study sites for the Nature Conservancy Wetland Network, a group of sites that scientists from around the world are working with to determine the quality of wetlands and their management for long-term health. The other two sites are the headwaters of the Amazon, in Peru, and the Great Salt Lake, in Utah.

A small, pristine lake called Lulu was purchased in 1992 by the Nature Conservancy. Around this time, one of the biologists on the Wisconsin Nature Conservancy board recognized the fen quality near this wetland and urged protection. The fen is one of the most rare wetland types left in Wisconsin.

By the opening of the twenty-first century the Nature Conservancy had managed to protect 1,100 acres through acquisitions and conservation easements with private landowners. "We're always aware that the only way long-term protection works is with heavy dependence on support of local communities," says Scott Thompson, director of Conservation, Eastern Wisconsin.

Thompson has his own theory of why the wetland I live beside managed to escape destruction. "Why tile a kettle?" he says. "The hills surrounding the wetland are too steep. The other barrier for early farming was the original oak trees along the hillsides, which were much more difficult to remove completely to plow and plant a crop." The soil itself was often sandy, which made it a problem for early house-building projects. Foundations, once dug, often collapsed.

One of the most important factors, says Thompson, was that the wetland in Section 13 had few owners, most of whom maintained their large tracts for many years. "They had what I would call a land ethic," says Thompson. "When we talk to the generation who owned the land often for thirty, forty, fifty years or more, what we find is that they speak fondly of the wetland and the river—where they went, how they hunted, fished, and swam here. They want to protect it."

Longtime landowners born and raised here, according to Thompson, often have a different viewpoint from people who come from the outside and do not have an outdoors orientation. "They've moved from cities or more congested suburban areas and have purchased a few acres and only want to keep out development."

Balancing the needs of these two groups, keeping channels of communication open while protecting the land, and educating about the value of what's here and how easily it can be destroyed are the biggest challenges the Conservancy faces in a time when Waukesha County is quickly being covered with parking lots, retail chains, and new housing developments.

Finding enough quality water is reaching crisis proportions— even in a region where so many small lakes abound. The shallow sandstone aquifer used by local municipalities is slowly being sucked dry. Some communities have already discovered radon in drinking water from deeper underground reservoirs. To remove radon is too costly for municipalities, so many town officials have supported projects to pipe water in from beyond their own localities. This situation will only further exasperate aquifer depletion.

"Building houses in flood plains, constructing driveways, roads, and parking lots over key recharge areas all take a toll on the way water filters into the ground," Thompson explains. "Whenever an area is paved or made into a parking lot, it effects water quality. It effects the way the groundwater is recharged."

When one part of the environment changes, another part is altered as well, says Thompson. "The whole thing is like a puzzle. You look at one aspect and then discover something else. Make a shift here, then a shift goes on there. Housing and commercial developers often don't take this into account. Towns eager for tax dollars and revenue often don't demand environmental impact studies from developers. They see short-term, not long-term effects."

He admits that one of the biggest challenges the Nature Conservancy faces is people's perceptions. It's easy to take a group out to look at an oak opening that the Nature Conservancy has preserved and managed. "People have no difficulty falling in love with oak trees. They don't get their feet muddy when they walk out among beautiful trees. You just look up, and there are the marvelous branches and leaves—familiar, reassuring," says Thompson. "It takes more effort to fall in love with a wetland. It takes even more effort to understand that what they can't see—the water beneath the ground we all take for granted—is directly impacted by the quality of the wetlands."

Many people, he says, continue to think of all marshes as nasty, buggy places "where the Creature of the Black Lagoon lives." Unlike early Native Americans, many modern Wisconsinites and other visitors won't go willingly into a wetland.

Respect and appreciation for wetlands are still relatively new ideas in America. Even the name "wetlands" was coined only as recently as 1956 by hydrologists working for the Federal Fish and Wildlife Service, who struggled for a number of years to come up with a meaningful definition. Not until the 1980s did the federal government, with support of scientists, take steps to actively stop wetland destruction.

At the threshold of the twenty-first century, environmental conservation groups and educators continue to attempt to increase the awareness of the public about the ecological value of wetlands. This effort remains an uphill battle. Draining and destruction of wetlands has not ceased, largely because of corporate greed and short-sighted, often destructive governmental policies.

For someone like Thompson, there is always hope—sometimes in the most unlikely places. "When I talk with some of the longtime landowners, what I quickly realize is that while they don't always know the names of all the particular wetland plants, they are eager to tell you, to show you what a special place the wetland is. They know the spot where lady's slippers grow at certain times of the year. They're aware of the places where their favorite birds nest."

It takes time and effort for people to acquire wetland familiarity and appreciation. It takes patience.

I ask him if he ever gets discouraged. Thompson laughs and nods. "Sometimes," he says. "Then I go down to the marsh. I hear cranes call."

# Epilogue

In Autumn dusk
cranes
carry my passion.
Hakyo (1913–1969)

I'd like to talk to the gossip who's been around long enough to hear all the stories, to witness all the comings and goings, births and deaths, romances and murders that have occurred in this wetland.

Someone has always lived here. The parade of residents throughout time is mindboggling—countless mastodons, mammoths, Paleoindians, elk, bears, Menominee, Potawatomi, Ho-Chunk, settlers, aphids, dragonflies, grasshoppers, herons—to name a few. I am only one of many creatures abiding here, passing through. The wetland does not belong to me or any other human being. It is a place shared by all living creatures. I am simply part of a community that resides here at the present moment.

Just as the creatures are always changing, always shifting, the land is constantly transforming. The wetland is continuously rearranging, altering from water to land to water and back again. In several thousand years, what will this place look like? I will never know.

It is unsettling at first to fully comprehend that nothing lasts forever. Not me, not the land around me, not anyone I hold dear. Everything is in a constant state of change. Accepting this fully means recognizing that my actions right now are all that I have to hold on to. *Present moment, wonderful moment.* That is all there is, but it is enough to make a difference.

Late afternoon and the sun is beginning to drop beneath the horizon. Along the northern edge of the lake I catch a glimpse of something brown wavering behind the sedges. I paddle closer, trying not to splash so that whatever it is won't become alarmed and flee.

A golden-eyed sandhill crane watches intruders carefully from the tall sedges.

Last rays of sun reflect on the lake and wetland.

Two half-hidden sandhill cranes wade into the calm, shallow water. I stop paddling and let the kayak drift and nose among the bulrush. I forget to breathe, I am holding so still. From where I crouch in the kayak, the top of my head is no higher than the birds' arched necks.

One crane, elegant as a dancer, lopes away. Water drips and glistens from each long, prehistoric leg as it retreats among the cattails. *Lift, drip, lift, drip.*

For some reason the other bird holds its ground. This is the closest I have ever been to a sandhill, close enough to see directly into its golden eyes. The crane's featherless bright red patch arches around its beak and eyes like a flamboyant mask. The effect is startling. Surrounded by brilliant red, the yellow eyes appear even more penetrating. The crane turns. With its long, slender beak now in profile, the bird pierces me with one searchlight eye.

I remember to breathe.

We gaze eye to eye for what seems a long time. Not moving, not afraid, not threatened—only curious. Our encounter is a respectful, straightforward appraisal of two living beings. "Aha!" we seem to say

An open fragrant water lily provides a handy landing site for winged insects.

to each other. "So that is who you are. You seem different from what I'd imagined."

I have become part of the crane's landscape. The crane has become part of my landscape as well.

And when the crane's examination of me seems complete, it swivels its head, crooks its long neck, and rests its beak against one rusty-colored wing. Calmly, the bird continues to observe me with its other eye, as if acknowledging that I bear watching but that I will do it no harm. This gesture of trust seems a kind of gift. In this single act, the crane—long a symbol of hope, transformation, and renewal—reiterates for me a powerful, important message. *We live here together, you and I.*

Gently, I dip one paddle into the water and push. The kayak skirts the bulrush and heads into the open lake. Wind ripples the surface. The cool, pungent air smells of distance, of freedom. As the last rays of sun vanish, I enter the mouth of the stream that leads back into the wetland.

# Bibliography

## Archives

Beach, Platt S. 1846 Correspondence. Archives. Manuscript collection. Folder SC 673 MAD 4/14/SC673. Wisconsin State Historical Society, Madison.

Brink, John M. Survey notes, maps, 1836. Interior vol. 161, exterior vol. 56, Troy Twp. Archives. Wisconsin Board of Commissioners of Public Lands, Madison.

Brown, Charles E. Papers, 1889–1945. MAD 4/19/C4–5, D1–4. Wisconsin MSS HB. Box 3, includes LeMere interview, 1911. Wisconsin State Historical Society, Madison.

Dwinnell, Solomon. Papers and Diaries 1775–1777, 1834–1879. WIS MSS CJ MAD 4/17/C3. Wisconsin State Historical Society, Madison.

Wisconsin Land Economic Inventory. Project material and field maps, 1929–1947. Archives. Final summary file, series 1956, box 63, 1936 inventory Section 13, series 1958, box 3. Walworth County. Wisconsin State Historical Society, Madison.

## Published Sources

Baker, Charles M. "Autobiography." *Wisconsin Historical Collections* 6 (1872): 465–76.

Beckwith, Albert Clayton. *History of Walworth County, WI.* Vols. 1–2. Indianapolis: B.F. Bowen and Co., 1912.

Bieder, Robert E. *Native American Communities in Wisconsin, 1600 to 1960.* Madison: University of Wisconsin Press, 1995.

Birmingham, Robert A. and Leslie E. Eisenberg. *Indian Mounds of Wisconsin.* Madison: University of Wisconsin Press, 2000.

# Bibliography

Bottomley, Edwin. "An English Settler in Pioneer Wisconsin: The Letters of Edwin Bottomley 1842–1850." *Wisconsin Historical Collections,* State Historical Society of Wisconsin, 25 (1918).

Brockman, Kay M., *Wildlife in Early Wisconsin.* Ed. A. W. Schorger, Stevens Point, Wisc.: Wildlife Society, 1982.

Borman, R. G. *Ground-Water Resources and Geology of Walworth County,* Information Circular Number 34. Madison: U.S. Geological and Natural History Survey, 1976.

Borman, Susan. *Through the Looking Glass: A Field Guide to Aquatic Plants.* Stevens Point, Wisc.: Department of Natural Resources and Wisconsin Lakes Partnership, 1997.

Caduto, Michael J. *Pond and Brook.* Hanover, N.H.: University Press of New England, 1990.

Carr, Archie. *Handbook of Turtles.* Ithaca, N.Y.: Cornell University Press, 1952.

Christoffel, Rebecca. *Snakes of Wisconsin.* Madison: Wisconsin Department of Natural Resources, Bureau of Endangered Species, 2000.

——. *Amphibians of Wisconsin.* Madison: Wisconsin Department of Natural Resources, Bureau of Endangered Species, 2001.

Clayton, Lee. *Pleistocene Geology of Waukesha County, Wisconsin.* Wisconsin Geological and Natural History Survey, Bulletin 99, 2001.

Curtis, John T. *The Vegetation of Wisconsin.* Madison: University of Wisconsin Press, 1971.

Dahl, Thomas E. *Wetlands: Losses in the United States 1780 to 1980.* Washington, D.C.: U.S. Department of the Interior, Fish and Wildlife Service, United States Government Printing Office, 1990.

Davidson, J. N. *In Unnamed Wisconsin.* Milwaukee: Silas Chapman, 1895.

Dick, Everett. *Lure of the Land.* Lincoln: University of Nebraska Press, 1970.

Donaldson, E. Talbot. *Beowulf: A New Prose Translation.* New York: W. W. Norton, 1966.

Edsall, Marian S. *Roadside Plants and Flowers.* Madison: University of Wisconsin Press, 1985.

Eggers, Steve D. *Wetland Plants and Plant Communities of Minnesota and Wisconsin.* St. Paul: U.S. Army Corps of Engineers, 1997.

Errington, Paul L. *Of Men and Marshes.* Ames: Iowa State University Press, 1996.

Gard, Robert E. *Wisconsin Lore.* New York: Duell, Sloan and Pearce, 1962.

Geib, W. J. "Soil Survey of Walworth County Wisconsin." Washington, D.C.: U.S. Department of Agriculture, Bureau of Soils, Government Printing Office, 1924.

Grooms, Steve. *The Cry of the Sandhill Crane.* Minocqua, Wisc.: North Word Press, 1992.

Hall, Robert L. "Red Banks, Oneota, and the Winnebago: Views From a Distant Rock." *Wisconsin Archeologist* 74 (1993): 10–79.

Hambrey, Michael. *Glaciers.* Cambridge: Cambridge University Press, 1992.

Hamerstrom, Frances. *Birds of Prey of Wisconsin.* Madison: Wisconsin Department of Natural Resources and Madison Audubon Society, 1983.

———. *Harrier Hawk of the Marshes.* Washington, D.C.: Smithsonian Press, 1986.

Harding, James H. *Amphibians and Reptiles of the Great Lakes Region.* Ann Arbor: University of Michigan Press, 2000.

Hathaway, Franklin. "Surveying in Wisconsin 1837." *Wisconsin Historical Collections* 15 (1892): 390–98.

Heinrich, Bernd. *Winter World: The Ingenuity of Animal Survival.* New York: HarperCollins, 2003.

Heist, Annette C. "Wisconsin Wetland Resources." *National Water Summary on Wetland Resources,* Report, U.S. Geological Survey Water-Supply Paper 2425. Washington, D.C.: Government Printing Office, 1996.

Hibbard, Benjamin. *A History of Public Land Policies.* New York: Peter Smith, 1939.

Highsmith, Hugh. *The Mounds of Koshkonong and Rock River.* Fort Atkinson, Wisc.: Highsmith Press, 1997.

Hill, Jen, Ed. *An Exhilaration of Wings: The Literature of Birdwatching.* New York: Penguin, 1999.

*History of Walworth County: Containing an Account of Its Settlement, Growth, Development and Resources.* Chicago: Western Historical Company, 1882.

Holman, J. Alan. *Ancient Life of the Great Lakes Basin.* Ann Arbor: University of Michigan Press, 1995.

———. *In Quest of Great Lakes Ice Age Vertebrates.* East Lansing: Michigan State University Press, 2001.

Hurley, William M. "The Late Woodland Stage: Effigy Mound Culture." *Wisconsin Archeologist.* 67,3–4 (1986): 283–392.

Josephy, Alvin M. Jr. *America in 1492: American Civilization on the Eve of the Columbus Voyages.* New York: Vintage Books, 1992.

Kemper, Jackson. "A Trip through Wisconsin in 1838." *Wisconsin Historical Collections* 6 (1872):465–76.

Korb, Randy M. *Wisconsin Frogs: Places to Hear Frogs and Toads near Our Urban Areas.* Green Bay: Northeastern Wisconsin Audubon, 2001.

Lapham, Increase Allen. *Wisconsin: Its Geography and Topography*. Milwaukee: I. A. Hopkins, 1846.

——. *The Antiquities of Wisconsin as Surveyed and Described*. Introduction by Robert P. Nurre. Madison: University of Wisconsin Press, 2001.

Lawlor, Elizabeth P. *Discover Nature in Water and Wetland*. Mechanicsburg, Pa.: Stackpole Books, 2000.

Lawrence, Gale. *A Field Guide to the Familiar: Learning to Observe the Natural World*. Hanover, N.H.: University Press of New England, 1998.

Leopold, Aldo. *A Sand County Almanac*. London: Oxford University Press, 1968.

Lurie, Nancy Oestreich. *Wisconsin Indians*. Madison: Wisconsin Historical Society Press, 2002.

Mallam, R. Clark. "Bears, Birds, Panthers, Elephants, and Archeologists: A Reply." *Wisconsin Archeologist* 61 (1980): 375–86.

Marryat, Frederick. "An English Officer's Description of Wisconsin in 1837." *Wisconsin Historical Collections* 14 (1891): 137–47.

Marshall, James. *Land Fever: Dispossession and Frontier Myth*. Lexington: University Press of Kentucky, 1986.

McBride, Genevieve G. *On Wisconsin Women: Working for Their Rights from Settlement to Suffrage*. Madison: University of Wisconsin Press, 1993.

Mills, Enos A. *In Beaver World*. Lincoln: University of Nebraska Press, 1990.

Niering, William A. *Wetlands*. New York: Alfred A Knopf, 1985.

Nero, Robert W. *Redwings*. Washington, D.C.: Smithsonian Press, 1984.

Olson, Sigurd F. *The Singing Wilderness*. Minneapolis: University of Minnesota Press, 1984.

Outwater, Alice. *Water: A Natural History*. New York: Basic Books, 1996.

Overstreet, David F. "Paleoindian Traditions in Southeastern Wisconsin: An Overview." *Wisconsin Archeologist* 72.3–4 (1991): 265–366.

Pielou, E. C. *After the Ice Age: The Return of Life to Glaciated North America*. Chicago: University of Chicago Press, 1991.

——. *Fresh Water*. Chicago: University of Chicago Press, 1998.

Price, Alice Lindsay. *Cranes: The Noblest Flyers*. Albuquerque, N.M.: La Alameda Press, 2001.

Prince, Hugh. *Wetlands of the American Midwest: A Historical Geography of Changing Attitudes*. Chicago: University of Chicago Press, 1997.

Quimby, George Irving. *Indian Life in Upper Great Lakes*. Chicago: University of Chicago Press, 1960.

Quinney, Richard. "A Place Called Home," *Wisconsin Magazine of History* 67, no. 3 (spring 1984): 163–84.

Radin, Paul. *Road of Life and Death: A Ritual Drama of the American Indians.* New York: Pantheon Books, 1945.

———. *The Trickster: A Study in American Indian Mythology.* New York: Schocken Books, 1972.

———. *The Winnebago Tribe.* Lincoln: University of Nebraska Press, 1990.

Risjord, Norman K. *Wisconsin: Story of the Badger State.* Madison: Wisconsin Trails, 1995.

Ritzenthaler, Pat, and Robert Ritzenthaler. *Woodland Indians of Western Great Lakes.* Prospect Heights, Ill.: Waveland Press, 1993.

Ryder, Hope. *Lily Pond: Four Years with a Family of Beavers.* New York: William Morrow, 1989.

Salzer, Robert J. "Oral Literature and Archeology." *Wisconsin Archeologist* 74.1–4 (1993): 80–119.

Sasso, Robert F., and Michelle Wilder. "A Preliminary Assessment of Nineteenth Century Potawatomi Agriculture and Land Use Practices in Southeastern Wisconsin." *Wisconsin Archeologist* 79.1 (1998): 185–207.

Schultz, Gwen. *Ice Age Lost.* Garden City, N.J.: Anchor/Doubleday, 1974.

*Selected Poems of William Carlos Williams.* Ed. Charles Tomlinson. New York: New Directions Books, 1985.

Skinner, Alanson. "Prairie Potawatomi Indians, Myths." *Bulletin of the Public Museum of the City of Milwaukee* 6–7 (1924–33): 332–59.

Smith, Dwight G. *Great Horned Owl.* Mechanicsburg, Pa.: Stackpole Books, 2002.

Smith, Huron H. *Ethnobotany of Menomini Indians.* Milwaukee Order of the Board of Trustees, *Bulletin of the Public Museum of the City of Milwaukee* 4, no. 1 (1923).

———. "Ethnobotany of the Forest Potawatomi." *Bulletin of the Public Museum of the City of Milwaukee* 7 (1933): 23–95.

Starin, Frederick J. "Diary of a Journey to Wisconsin." *Wisconsin Magazine of History* 5–6 (1923–34): 73–95, 207–30.

Stephenson, Isaac. *Recollections of a Long Life.* Chicago: Private Printing, 1915.

Stokes, Donald. *Nature in Winter.* Boston: Little, Brown and Company, 1976.

Stoltman, James B. "Paleoindian Adaptive Strategies in Wisconsin during Late Pleistocene Times." *Wisconsin Archeologist* 79.1 (1998): 53–67.

Strong, Moses. *History of Wisconsin Territory.* Madison: Democratic Printing, 1885.

Strong, Paul. *Beavers: Where Waters Run.* Minocqua, Wisc.: North Word Press, 1997.

Tekiela, Stan. *Wildflowers of Wisconsin.* Cambridge, Minn.: Adventure Publications, 2000.

Thayer, Crawford B., ed. *Hunting for a Shadow: The Search for Black Hawk.* Fort Atkinson, Wisc: Banta Press, 1981.

U.S. Department of Agriculture, Bureau of Soils. *Soil Survey of Walworth County, Wisconsin,* W.J. Geib, ed. Washington, D.C.: Government Printing Office, 1924.

Van Wormer, Joe. *World of Canada Goose.* New York: J. B. Lippincott, 1968.

Vileisis, Ann. *Discovering the Unknown Landscape: A History of America's Wetlands.* Washington, D.C.: Island Press, 1997.

Vliet, John B. "The Story of a Wisconsin Surveyor." *Wisconsin History Magazine* 8 (1924–25): 57–66.

Warner, Mrs. Ambrose. "Recollections of Farm Life." *Wisconsin Historical Collections* 6 (1872): 193–203.

Weller, Milton W. *Freshwater Marshes: Ecology and Wildlife Management.* Minneapolis: University of Minnesota Press, 1994.

White, C. Albert. *A History of the Rectangular Survey System.* Washington, D.C.: U.S. Department of the Interior, 1983.

Wright, D. E. *Place of the Bear: History of Mukwanago.* Mukwanago: Private printing, 1994.

# Index